DATE DUE

GAYLORD			PRINTED IN U.S.A.

foxtails, ferns, & fish scales

by Ada Graham

illustrated by Dorothea Stoke

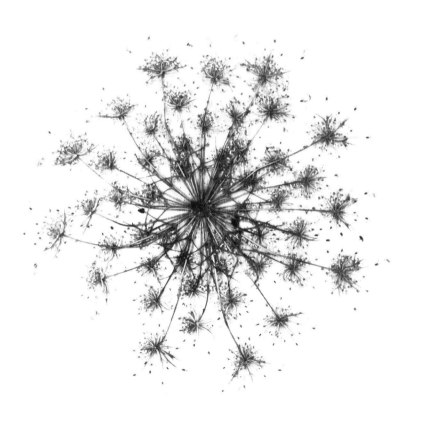

foxtails, ferns, & fish scales:

A Handbook of Art and Nature Projects

Four Winds Press
New York

For Tim, Jennifer, Jon, and the two Franks

The activities in this book were all carried out by
Tim at age twelve and Jennifer at age ten. Many of
Tim's and Jennifer's prints and projects are included
here as well as those of their mother, who is the
illustrator of this book.

Library of Congress Cataloging in Publication Data

Graham, Ada.
  Foxtails, ferns, and fish scales.

  Bibliography: p.
  SUMMARY: Suggestions for craft projects using materials
such as algae, leaves, and seeds collected outdoors.
  1. Natural history—Outdoor books—Juvenile literature.
2. Handicraft—Juvenile literature. [1. Nature study. 2. Handi-
craft] I. Stoke, Dorothea.
II. Stoke, Jon. III. Title.
QH48.G74   745.5   76–17131
ISBN 0–590–07378–8

Published by Four Winds Press
A Division of Scholastic Magazines, Inc., New York, N.Y.
Copyright © 1976 by Ada Graham and Dorothea Stoke
All rights reserved
Printed in the United States of America
Library of Congress Catalog Card Number: 76–17131
1   2   3   4   5   80   79   78   77   76

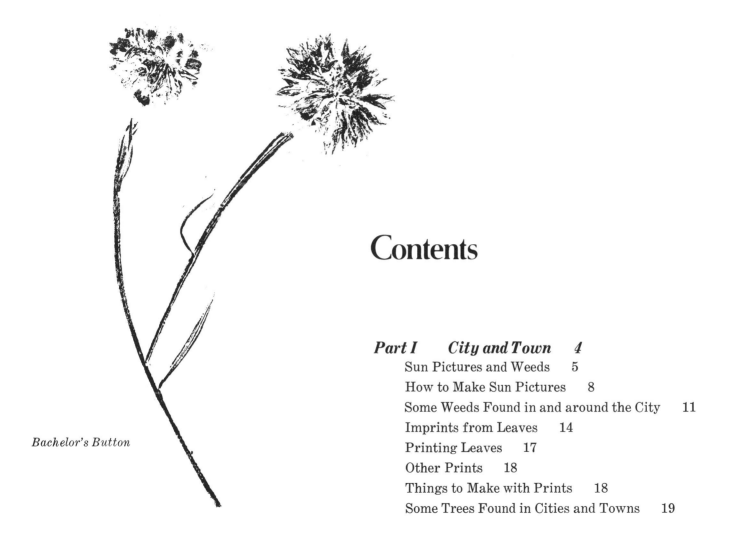

Bachelor's Button

Contents

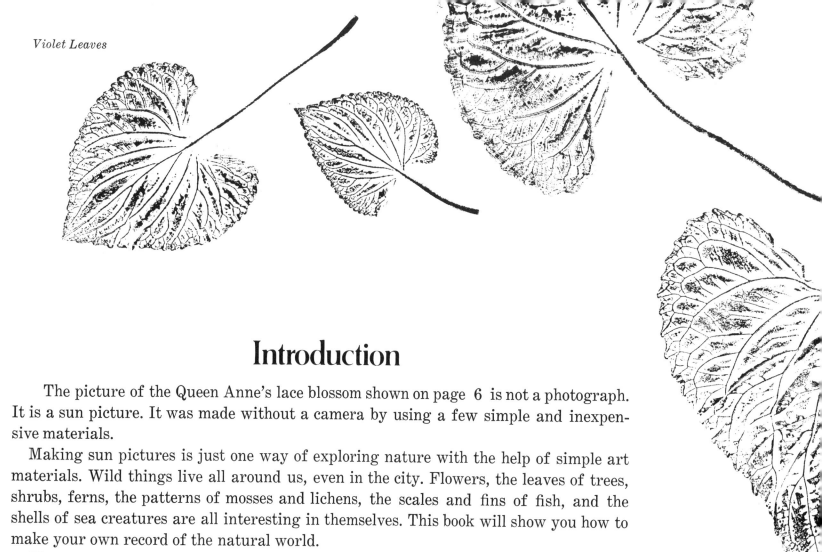

Violet Leaves

Introduction

The picture of the Queen Anne's lace blossom shown on page 6 is not a photograph. It is a sun picture. It was made without a camera by using a few simple and inexpensive materials.

Making sun pictures is just one way of exploring nature with the help of simple art materials. Wild things live all around us, even in the city. Flowers, the leaves of trees, shrubs, ferns, the patterns of mosses and lichens, the scales and fins of fish, and the shells of sea creatures are all interesting in themselves. This book will show you how to make your own record of the natural world.

The shapes and textures of wild things are often pleasing to see and feel. We enjoy working with them, displaying or duplicating their most attractive features. And when

we have finished—when we have printed the pattern of a leaf or made a mobile from weathered driftwood—we are uniquely rewarded. We see details in the object we never noticed before and get clues to the story of its life in nature.

One of the purposes of this book is to help you to make interesting and attractive objects with natural materials. But collecting and working with these materials can be even more rewarding if you know something about the lives that produced them. You may find two objects lying side by side on the beach. One is a plastic container, the other a sand dollar. How much more interesting it is to learn a little bit about the sand dollar, find out how it came to be there, and work it into a meaningful composition that says something about its history.

Once you begin collecting and working with natural objects, you will see more than the objects themselves. You will see that the life of each one is tuned to the cycle of the year. The world around us changes with the seasons, wherever we live.

Plants put forth buds, the buds unfold into flowers and leaves, the flowers produce seeds, and the seeds scatter to produce new plants. Tiny animals hatch, grow, change their forms, and produce new animals of their own kind. This variety in nature turns your hobby into an endless adventure.

In making a record of this change, you will change and grow, too. You will begin to see the world around you more clearly. What you notice about a flower's form and structure and how you make use of it in a print or a composition will be different from the way anyone else sees it.

1

city and town

Sun Pictures and Weeds

When you walk on the sidewalk, do you ever see tiny plants growing from the cracks? Weeds of all kinds—chicory, sunflowers, dandelions, clover—grow wherever there is a little soil. They line the sides of a building, carpet empty lots, and spring up in the wells of earth left around trees on the streets.

Wild plants are so common in the city we rarely ever notice them. There are many different kinds and they are everywhere. Los Angeles has over one hundred and thirty different kinds of wild plants. Denver, in the mountains, has sixty, while in New York between the months of April and November you can find at least ninety species.

The variety in the shapes and outlines of the leaves alone gives you a wide selection with which to work. The tiny three-lobed clover leaves are very different from the more elaborate, branching ragweed. A dandelion leaf, the most common of all, has a very dramatic outline. The French named it *dent-de-lion*, meaning the teeth of the lion. Some experts think that is how

Queen Anne's Lace

the dandelion got its English name.

Leaves, although they are pretty enough in themselves, are not the only part of a plant that makes good sun pictures. As spring moves toward summer, flowers of many shapes begin to appear. Look again along the sides of buildings and in empty lots for the dominant colors, yellow and white, sometimes interspersed with blue or pink.

You will find in the city the umbrella-shaped blossom of the Queen Anne's lace, the little flower heads of clovers, the petals of chicory and sunflowers. Each will form a different pattern on your picture.

Some flowers will be tiny and hard to see. There is a reason for that. Not many insects visit wild flowers in the city. The flowers do not need bright and showy blossoms to attract bees and moths to pollinate them. The wind pollinates most of these flowers.

The tiny blossoms are heavy with pollen that is blown to the reproductive part of another blossom. You may see some of the yellow dust fall from the plant when you pick it. Tiny blossoms make interesting pictures too.

Once they are fertilized, these tiny blossoms become complicated seed packages. The fuzzy dandelion head gives you a good idea of the number of seeds each plant must produce to insure its survival. The heart-shaped capsules of the shepherd's purse, which give the plant its name, and the "bird's nest" flower head in which Queen Anne's lace holds its seeds are two very different kinds of seed packages. These packages make some of the most interesting sun pictures because

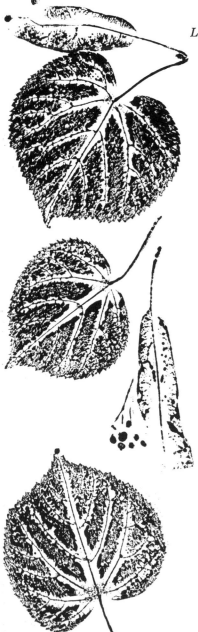

they tell a lot about the life of the weed you have found. Weeds are everywhere because they are able to produce so many seeds and distribute them so efficiently.

How to Make Sun Pictures

Making sun pictures is a kind of photography.

When photographers want to see what is on a negative, they often make a temporary print of it, using a sheet called studio proof paper. This paper is sensitive to light and darkens when it is exposed to sunlight. It is usually sold in boxes of twenty-five sheets at photo supply stores. If your store doesn't have it, ask them to order it for you.

While you are at the supply store, also buy a box of fixer. The studio proof paper on which you will make your sun pictures continues to darken when it is exposed to sunlight. You must fix it or stop it from developing any further or the picture will become so dark you cannot see it. The box of fixer contains the directions for mixing it. The only other equipment you need to make sun pictures is two long, shallow pans. They must be large enough to hold a sheet of studio proof paper. One pan will hold the fixer, the other will hold water for washing your picture.

Walk around your neighborhood on a sunny day. Almost any time of the year provides the plant material for a sun picture. Spring leaves, summer flowers, autumn seed coverings, and the dried, twisted plants of winter all make interesting pictures. Unlike rare woodland wild flowers, common weeds may be picked because they replace themselves easily.

Collect a variety of subjects for your sun pictures. Find plants of different sizes and shapes. Place them on a table away from the sunlight. Have the box of paper nearby, but do not take it out of the box yet. Now you are ready to try this special kind of photography.

First, prepare the fixer in one of the shallow pans. Fill the other pan with water. Then take a sheet of studio proof paper from the box and compose your picture on it, using one or more of the plants you collected.

Put the paper with your composition on a book or piece of cardboard to keep it steady. Carry it to the window and put it in direct sunlight. The sun will begin al-

most at once to darken the paper. The picture itself will be where the plant's leaves, branches, or flowers have blocked off the light.

When the paper turns a dark purple, it has reached its proper exposure. Carry it out of the light, remove the plant, and set the paper in the fixer. Leave it there for about five minutes to make sure it is fixed. Then put it in the water for ten minutes.

Meanwhile, you can be making other

Linden

sun pictures. Try other compositions. Move your plant around on the paper to get different effects. You may also want to vary the exposure time or remove parts of the arrangement at different times while it is still in the sunlight. Then you will get different patterns and shades. You may put several sheets of paper in the pans of fixer and water at the same time.

When the prints are finished, lay them on newspaper to dry. The proof paper curls somewhat while it is drying. When the pictures are thoroughly dry, press them in a book, or beneath some other heavy object to flatten them.

The sun pictures in this book were glued to a heavy backing that is used to mount pictures. It shows them off very well, and they can be displayed or dis-

tributed as gifts. Mat board can be purchased at an art supply shop. Sometimes picture framers have scraps that are the perfect size for this project. They will sell them to you at a saving. You may have too many pictures to treat in this special way and want to mount only the ones that appeal to you most.

Your pictures can include not only weeds but also leaves, fruits, berries, all kinds of flowers, butterflies, seaweeds, and sea creatures found at the beach. But the variety of weeds offers a great selection wherever you are.

Shepherd's Purse

Ragweed

Red Clover

Some Weeds Found in and around the City

Shepherd's purse came to America from Europe. The flowers are white and turn into wedge-shaped, somewhat flat seed capsules. They look to many people like an old-fashioned shepherd's purse.

Wild mustard has yellow flowers. There are many kinds of mustard and some of them provide the flavoring used in making commercial mustard.

Ragweed is sometimes called hay fever weed. If you get hay fever, don't pick this pollen-packed plant. Birds like the oil-rich seeds.

11

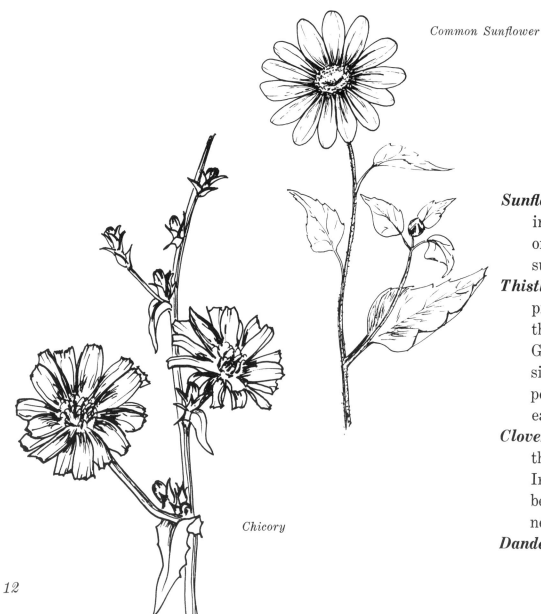

Common Sunflower

Chicory

Sunflower is a native plant that is present in nearly every state. There are over one hundred different kinds. Wild sunflower seeds are birds' favorites.

Thistles have pink flowers with spiny, prickly leaves. The seeds are carried through the air on tiny parachutes. Goldfinches love the seeds. A pretty sight is a yellow-and-black goldfinch perched on a bending thistle plant, eating its seeds.

Clovers are very common. One kind has the three-part leaf that is called the Irish shamrock. You will often see bees landing on clover flowers. Clover nectar makes good honey.

Dandelion is a very useful plant. Birds

like the seeds. People eat the tender green leaves in salads and make wine from the blossoms.

Lamb's-quarters is also called goosefoot because its leaves are said to resemble the feet of geese. It is very common. The tender leaves are cooked like spinach. The flowers are tiny, but the seeds are numerous.

Chicory has large attractive blue flowers. It is also called coffeeweed. It was used to make a coffee substitute in times of war when real coffee was not available.

Knotweed grows in a low mat. It makes an attractive pattern, branching out over the ground. The flowers are tiny.

Alfalfa

Dandelion

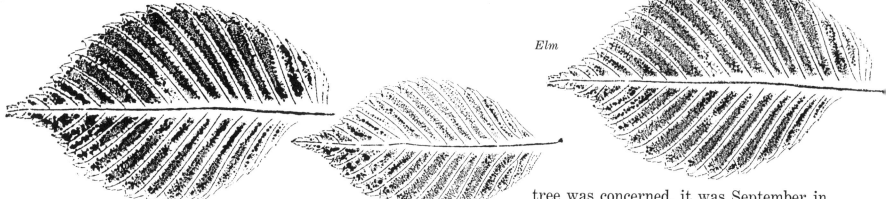

Elm

Imprints from Leaves

A tree scientist was telling a group of foresters a story about the adventures of a city tree.

Each fall, when all the other trees were losing their leaves, one tree on the street stood out. Its leaves held on stubbornly. The London plane tree's leaves blew in the wind far into December, puzzling everyone who walked by.

Scientists suspected the cause of the tree's confusion, but they did some investigating to make certain. They found that a steam line ran through the pit in which the tree had been planted! As far as this tree was concerned, it was September in December.

Trees face many difficulties in cities. The maze of underground pipes and wires interferes with root systems. The dense fumes from cars and buses clog the breathing systems of leaves. Smoke from factories kills many kinds of trees.

The trees you see growing along city streets were planted there because they are able to live with these many hazards. They come from countries all over the world and make leaf finding in the city a kind of worldwide tour. But they have one thing in common—all but the evergreens lose their leaves each fall.

Many changes take place in trees at that time. Drops in temperature and de-

creases in the amount of daylight warn the tree that the season is changing. The adhesive substance that glues the leaf stem to the twig dries up. When this happens, the leaves no longer receive nourishment from the tree or send any back to it.

The leaves stop making the chlorophyll which colors them green. The other colors that are in the leaf, but not visible, begin to show through now that the chlorophyll is gone. For instance, in trees that make a lot of sugar, chemicals turn the leaves red. The winds and rains follow, causing the drying leaves to flutter and fall to the ground.

When the leaves fall, they are no longer useful to the tree. The leaf you find lying on the ground, though, was alive and working a short time ago. The tree it came from was sending as much as a ton of water a day up the trunk and out to its leaves. The leaves, in turn, were catching sunlight and turning it into food for the tree. It is all this history that makes a leaf such a good subject for printing.

As you begin to handle leaves, not only will you notice the contrasts in their outlines, but you will also become conscious of their systems of veins. Veins cover most of a leaf's surface, dividing its area into equal parts. The veins of different kinds of leaves vary in thickness and they branch off at different angles.

These variations among leaf structures reveal their engineering. It is the way the tree has found to best bring water to every part of the leaf. Scientists have found that the thicker the main vein is, the smaller the angle of branching will be. The thinner the veins, the wider the angle of branching. Much of a leaf's history can be captured by printing it.

Printing Leaves

Simple equipment for experimenting with leaves and their structure can be purchased at any store that carries art supplies. You will find more details about this equipment in an appendix in the back of the book. But to start, you will need a roller or brayer and a tube of water-soluble printing ink, preferably black.

A pane of glass on which to roll the ink is the only other equipment you need. If you do not have a piece of clear glass, like that used in windows, buy one at a hardware store. A pane eight inches by twelve inches will be big enough for most leaves you wish to print. Put tape around the edges to keep the glass from breaking and cutting you.

Cover the table with several layers of newspaper. Lay out the leaves you have collected, the glass, ink, brayer, and paper for printing. Cheap paper is very good because it is absorbent.

Squeeze some ink on the glass. Roll it in one direction with the brayer, then in another until the ink sounds sticky. Lay the leaf on the inked glass with the veins down. Cover with a clean scrap of paper or newspaper and press it firmly into the ink. Rub the complete surface and veins of the leaf to make certain it is fully inked. Lift the paper and remove the leaf from the ink.

Lay the leaf, inked-side down, on a clean sheet of paper on which you wish to print. Cover the leaf and the paper with a clean sheet and press the leaf firmly with your fingers. (See instructions for printing in appendix.) Follow the structure of the veins out to the points of the leaf. This will insure a clear print. Feeling the leaf in this way will also make you familiar with the leaf's structure. Raise the paper and the leaf and examine the print.

A too dark print will require less ink, a too light one a bit more on the next printing. The same leaf can be printed over and over. Other leaves can be added to the page making a composition of the leaves. You will enjoy the contrast between the tiny fanlike shape of the ginkgo, with its veins all radiating outward, and the huge compound leaf of the ailanthus.

Other Prints

All of the weeds discussed in this book can be printed. Flowers and leaves with a flatter shape will give better results. Follow the same plan as for leaves.

Things to Make with Prints

Prints of ginkgo leaves, shepherd's purse, chicory, London plane tree leaves and three-leaf clover will make attractive placemats and notepaper.

The paper for both can be found in a ten-cent store, a hardware store, or the housewares section of a department store. A pad of drawing paper measuring twelve by eighteen inches is the right size for place mats. If you want to protect the mat, buy some pieces of clear contact paper. It can be sealed over the mat, making it washable.

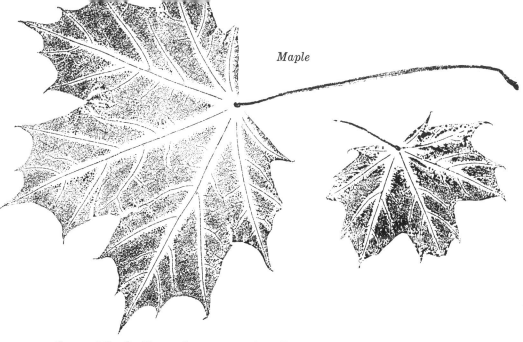

Maple

Any plain notepaper can be printed with weeds or leaves. A variety of forms makes an attractive package. Pads of paper that come with matching envelopes can be folded into note-size paper.

A picture of printed leaves or flowers can be mounted in the same way as sun pictures. Mounted on mat board, a leaf print makes an attractive reminder of the most colorful season of the year.

Some Trees Found in Cities and Towns

London plane tree comes to American cities from large cities in Europe. The trunk is spotted. The seeds are contained in balls with spines on them. The balls make attractive decorations.

Ailanthus is called tree of heaven in one of the oriental languages. It was brought to American cities from China. It grows like a weed and you will see it wherever you go. Its leaves are long and branchlike with many leaflets, and they fall from the branch in one piece. Its fruit looks somewhat like an airplane propeller.

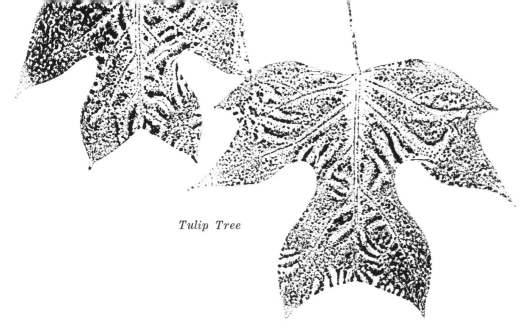

Tulip Tree

Ginkgo, also called maidenhair tree, is a living fossil. Its leaves are fern leaves from the age of reptiles. The veins of the leaves lie in the shape of a fan. Its fruit has a strong odor, somewhat like very old cheese. It was brought to cities from China. Scientists have found that it withstands car and bus exhaust better than most other trees.

Honey locust is native to the states of Kentucky, Ohio, and Tennessee. It grows well in cities and is very decorative. The leaves are jagged and lacelike, cut on the edges and are composed of several leaflets. The trunk has spines on it. It is not a good tree for climbing.

Horse chestnut has very large seven-part leaves that look something like pinwheels. Because they are large, they make a dramatic print. The fruit is a nut contained in a spiny husk, and it is inedible. This tree comes from Rumania in southeast Europe.

Maple leaf is one of the most commonly known shapes. You may see members of this family wherever you go.

Norway maple is one of the most commonly seen maples. It is very resistant to smoke and, as the name implies, came from northern Europe.

Box elder is a maple that is native to America. It grows in cities and towns.

You can recognize it as a maple because of the characteristic two-winged seeds which all maples have.

Oak family is the largest group of native American trees. Over two hundred kinds occur in this country. All oaks have acorns, but some produce them only every other year. Oak leaves are deeply cut and pointed and are always longer than they are wide.

American elm was a tree of the American woods and was brought to cities and planted on streets because it is tall and stately. You will not see as many of these trees as you would have in the past because they are being killed by a disease.

Flowering trees are planted in parks, in front of buildings, and in yards for their lovely spring blossoms. Cherry, crabapple, and hawthorn are all lovely to look at in spring.

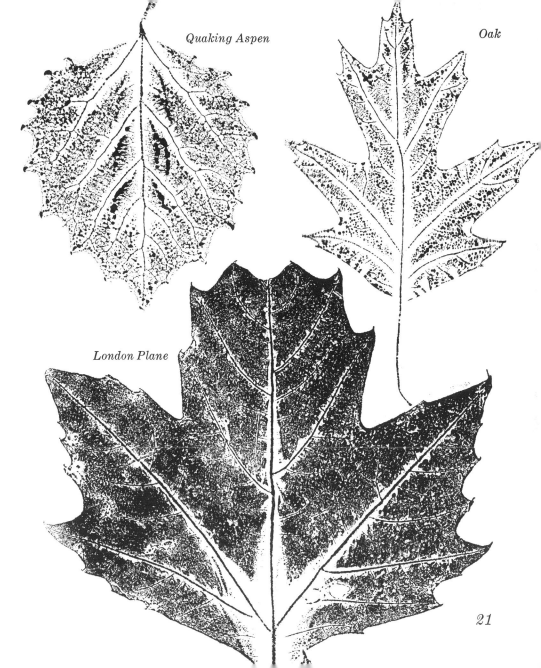

Quaking Aspen

Oak

London Plane

21

Fish Printing

The ice in the fish store window is covered with fish of many kinds. The fins are spread out, the scales glisten. It is easy to imagine the living fish using various fins to control its body for a quick attack or a speedy escape.

As we look at them now, we can picture the variety of fish darting in and out among the plants and boulders of the

22

ocean depths they so recently inhabited. You may see the shad that swam up rivers to lay eggs, the sardines or herring, the cod and pollack that were pulled up by huge draggers in the cold northern waters. You may find snapper, snook, porgies, or catfish, taken from southern waters and shipped to markets all over the country.

Holding and turning the fish and examining its shape that is streamlined for speed help you to imagine the kind of life the fish may have led. Tracing its scales in the intricate patterns they make over the fish's back and sides, finding where the fins are attached, folding them out, opening its mouth, and examining the shape of its head can tell you more about a fish than any book. And capturing these details on paper tells you even more.

Nearly all fish have fins. They are lo-cated on different parts of the body and do different jobs. The tail fin is used to steer and probe, while two other fins in the rear, called pelvic fins, produce stability and lift, as the tail wings of an airplane do.

All the fins are movable and are worked by muscles in the fish's body. The two sets of front fins, the pectoral and dorsal, work together to provide stability. The pectorals, just behind the gills, reach out sideways and are used for turning. The dorsals stand straight up on the fish's back, keeping it vertical. When reproduced with ink on paper, the fins give a sense of life and movement.

The tiny mirrors covering the surface of the fish, the scales, give the fish an irregular texture that makes an interesting print. Scales cover a fish's body just as feathers cover a bird's. As you print different fish, you will notice that scales are not always alike. There are several kinds. The most common kind has sharp teeth at one end. Scales grow as the fish grows, and they grow faster in summer than in winter. Like trees, they form rings, narrow or wide, by which the fish's age can be told.

How to Print Fish

Buy a fish that interests you at a fish store or the fish counter of a supermarket. The ink you will use can be washed off with cold water, and the fish can be eaten when you have finished printing it.

Make certain the head and tail are left on the fish. If the fish is cleaned, or has its insides removed, at the store, ask the clerk to make only a small slit in its body. It will be easier to control the shape of the fish if the slit is small.

At an art supply shop ask for a pad of newsprint. Newsprint comes in large sheets, is inexpensive and prints well. Another paper that makes good prints is shelf paper. It comes in rolls. You can find it in a supermarket.

Rice paper makes an especially good print. When you want to keep a print, use this special paper. It is more expensive than the others. Buy a few sheets large enough to take a print of the entire fish. For many centuries people in the island country of Japan have used rice paper to make fish prints. Some of those prints are so beautiful they are in museums.

Wash the fish with a mild soapy solution. This removes the fish's surface slime which protects it from disease. Dry the fish thoroughly, all the time looking at it carefully. Study the parts of the fish you wish to capture on your print. Look at its shape, the size and placement of the fins, the pattern of the scales, and the shape of the head.

Stuff pieces of cotton or tissue in the cavity from which its organs were taken and in its mouth. This will keep any liquid still on the inside from leaking out.

The gills, or openings behind the head, may also leak. Put some cotton or tissue in them at the same time. Look for a tiny vent, or hole, near the tail and plug it too.

A flat fish is easiest to print. If yours is plump, you may have to roll up some paper and place it under the fish to keep it from slipping while you are printing it. Spread out the fins and the tail. They are collapsible, like an old-fashioned fan.

Roll the ink across the surface of the fish, running the roller from the head to the tail. Otherwise, you may disturb the

Flounder

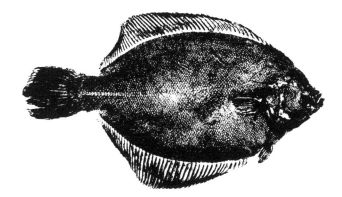

25

position of the scales. Take some extra time to see that the head is inked completely, as well as the fins and tail.

Lay the paper over the fish and begin to explore all of the fish's surface with your fingers. Run your fingers around its head, over the pattern of scales, and along each fin, capturing as many details as possible. Lift your print and examine it. You may be surprised by its wonderful detail.

Continue making prints, using more or less ink and more or less rubbing, until you get results that particularly satisfy you. Then try making a print with the rice paper.

After printing your fish a number of times you may find that its scales have become clogged with ink. Then, instead of getting a print of the scales, you may be getting only more ink. If this happens, wash off the ink and dry and stuff the fish once again.

Don't forget, when you are finished printing, wash off all the ink. The fish can then be cooked and eaten.

Some Common Fish that Can Be Printed

trout of all kinds	mackerel
cod	skate
pollack	catfish
flounder	bass
shad	snapper
herring	porgy

2

the side of the road

The Side of the Road

The intricate design you see here is the web of an orb-weaving spider. This spider is a member of a community of plants and animals that lives in grassy areas along the sides of roads.

Roads are more than tar, concrete, and speed limits. They have borders which are filled with stands of colorful roadside flowers. The flowers attract nectar-seeking insects. Small birds and animals come to feed on the insects and later on the seeds of the flowers.

This narrow band of roadside life is a rich area for collecting and observing.

Orb-Weaving Spiders

Spiders build structures that interest both scientists and artists. Fortunately for all of us who delight in spider webs, the world's largest family of spiders is also that which builds orb webs. Not all spiders build webs.

Some of the best times to enjoy webs are early mornings, when they are covered with dew, after summer showers, or on foggy days. Droplets of moisture glisten on the lines of the web. But spider webs are worth watching at any time. If you watch the web closely you may get a glimpse of its builder.

Many orb-weaving spiders roll up in a leaf nearby, hiding from the insects on which they prey. A direct line from the hub of the web to the hidden spider transmits vibrations made by insects caught in the web.

Some spider watchers suggest cutting a part of the web gently with a blade of grass, then waiting silently. The spider might come out and repair it before your very eyes! But remain still. Spiders are very shy creatures and will flee from any movement.

It takes approximately an hour for a spider to build one of nature's more com-plicated wonders. A lot of web building is done at night. The spider's thousands of tiny spinnerets provide the silk from which the web is constructed.

The spider starts by making a bridge. Usually a line is blown out from the spinneret and attaches itself to another point. The spider than walks across this bridge and drops a second line, anchoring it

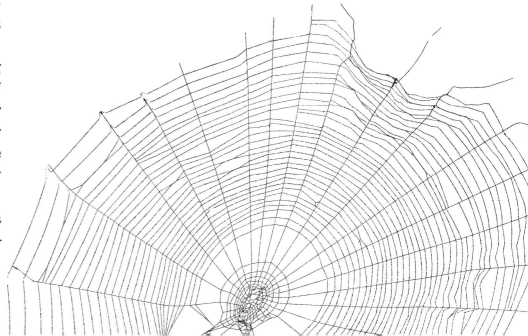

Captured Spider Web

firmly. Now it returns to what will be the center, or hub, of the web. Radial threads, those stretching from the center outward, are carried from the hub to the bridge.

When the orb weaver begins to make the spirals, those lines linking one radial thread to another, its leg touches the previous spiral before beginning a new round. In that way the spider measures the distance between spirals.

This is only a temporary spiral. When it is finished, the spider reverses itself. It eats the old spiral as it proceeds toward

the center and puts a more closely spaced one in its place. This gives the web greater strength.

Spiders work hard at keeping the web in repair. Some part of it needs to be mended daily. Spiderlings know instinctively how to build webs. Researchers have found, however, that their ability to make webs improves with experience.

Spider Pictures

Spider pictures are easy to make and are a reminder of the times you spent spider watching.

Buy a small can of black spray paint such as Rustoleum or any other brand that does not contain the spray propellant

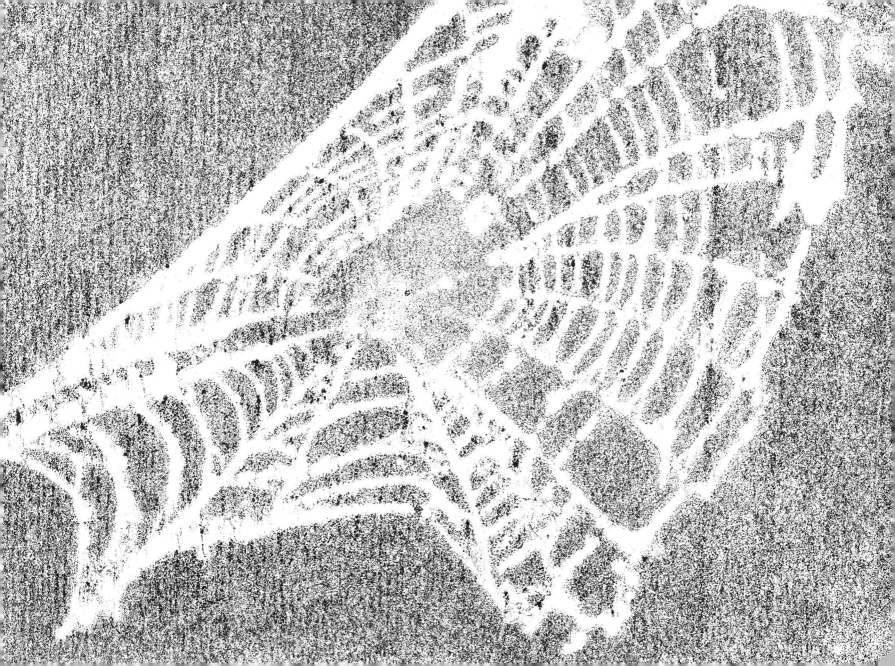

known as fluorocarbon or Freon. You will find a list of the can's contents on the label. Many scientists believe that fluorocarbons are harmful to the environment.

You will also need a piece of mat board or stiff paper such as oak tag on which to collect your spider picture. Carry some old newspapers to protect the surrounding plants from the spray paint.

Spider webs are abundant in the fields along roads. When you find an attractive one, examine it carefully. Locate the lines that anchor the web to the surrounding vegetation. They are called guidelines. You will need to know where they are later.

Hold the newspaper behind the web. It is useful to have a helper to hold the paper for you.

Start spraying paint at the center of the web, moving outward around the spirals. In this way you will not miss any of the lines. When the lines are completely covered, move the newspaper to the opposite side and spray again. Spraying both sides will help to adhere the web to the board.

Hold the stiff paper or board firmly. Look for the guidelines and loosen or cut them. Move the paper upright toward the web, with one hand behind it for support, capturing the web on the paper as you move. Allow it to dry for ten minutes before touching.

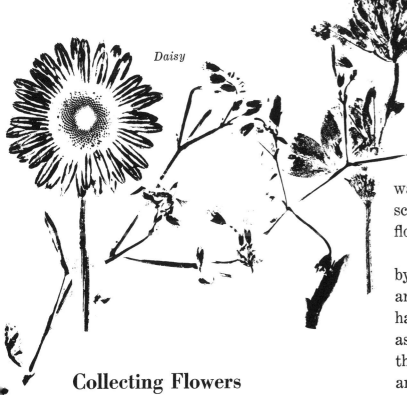

Daisy

Wild Rose

Collecting Flowers

Early Americans used wild plants in many ways. They ate dandelions, wild onions, garlic, and parsnips. They made seasonings from wild mustard, caraway, and mint. They found cures for backaches from gill-over-the-ground. Heal-all was used to close open wounds, and skin lotion was made of butter-and-eggs. Rose petals scented blanket chests, and a variety of flowers were used to dye natural wool.

The colonists called all the wild flowers by name—rattlebox, crowfoot, cowbane, and buttefly weed. They recognized plants harmful to them and their animals, such as lambkill. It is pleasant to be reminded that we are looking at the same flowers and calling them by the same vivid names as colonial Americans did. These same flowers grow plentifully along the sides of our roads today.

Each flower blooms only to be fertilized. The female egg cell of each flower must make contact with the male sperm cells of another flower of its own kind to insure its survival. Insects are plentiful in fields and along roadsides, and the many-colored flowers attract bees, pollinating beetles, and butterflies to complete this vital process.

Some flowers such as buttercups, which belong to flower families of older geologic periods, have simple parts. Newer families have found ways of making it easier for birds and insects to fertilize them.

As flowers changed, they came to have special features to attract insects to them. They developed what are called honey guides, which lead insects quickly and efficiently to the male sperm cells or pollen.

Converging bright eyespots on the petals, rows of dots, or the shape of the flower itself guides the insect to its goal. In addition, the yellow-orange, blue-purple, red-pink, and white colors of the flowers correspond to special color-sensitive insects. Bees are thought to be more sensitive to blue-purple and yellow flowers, while butterflies are more conscious of red-orange blossoms. Looking at a flower from an insect's point of view is an interesting hobby. Each flower becomes a puzzle, with answers hidden in the journey it makes as it becomes next year's seed.

Pressing Flowers

Picking flowers is a pleasant activity and it becomes more enjoyable when you know you are going to use the flowers you pick. There are pictures in museums made from dried flowers that are hundreds of years old. Some herbarium sheets in museums, holding and labeling the dried flowers, are 300 years old and in good condition.

All you need for collecting and drying flowers are several sheets of old newspaper. Newspaper is used to make folded pads to absorb the moisture.

Here are some tips for drying flowers:

Gather leaves of the flowers as well as the flowers themselves. They make attractive pictures.

When you put the flowers and leaves between the sheets, as you would between the pages of a book, spread them out and separate them as much as possible. Do not bunch them one on top of another.

When collecting, take long stems. You can always cut them later.

It sometimes helps to smooth the flowers

carefully with your fingers and even press them gently with your hand. This is especially true if the flower head is thick and heavy.

Do not try to crowd too many plants on one sheet. Use several sheets.

When all your plants are placed between the sheets of the newspaper pad, find a dry spot to store them. Cover the paper with a layer of books. The weight will press the plants and keep them from shrinking. They will be completely dry in about a week. You may look at them at any time to check them. The dried material can be kept for a long time. You can use it the following winter if you wish. Some people take the flowers from between the sheets and store them in boxes. You now have material with which to work.

Using Dried Flowers

Gluing

To make a flower picture:

Assemble a bottle of Elmer's glue, a paint brush, water, a plain piece of paper, a stiff background such as a mat board used for mounting pictures, and your dried flowers.

Compose a picture of the dried flowers on the plain piece of paper. This gives you a chance to move them around and change them before gluing. Mix enough Elmer's glue and water in equal quantities to cover the entire surface of the stiff background you plan to use for your picture.

With the brush, apply the glue and water lightly over the entire surface.

Brush the back of each of the plants with the mixture before you transfer them, one by one, to the board. When the flowers are flat, press them lightly with the tips of your fingers. Lay aside to dry. You may want to add a border to your flower picture with a magic marker and a ruler. You now have a picture ready for hanging.

Pressing between Contact Paper

To make postcards, bookmarks, and stationery:

Another way to use your pressed flowers is to preserve them under a layer of contact paper. Contact paper comes in clear sheets or rolls. You can buy it in the housewares section of a large depart-

ment store, a ten-cent store, or a hardware store.

To make postcards you will need unlined index cards, four inches by six inches, and contact paper. Cut the contact paper the same size as the postcards. Lay out your dried flowers and leaves on the cards.

There are two ways you can press the flowers beneath the paper. You can lay the flowers on the postcard and cover them with the paper. Or you can lay the flowers on the sticky contact paper, press them down, and cover with the card. Rub your fingers firmly around the flowers and

leaves. This embeds the flower in the plastic and it stands out more clearly.

If you cover the card with enough flowers and leaves to fill about two-thirds of its surface you will usually get a pleasing composition. More flowers will make the card look too crowded. Fewer flowers will make it look a bit empty.

When the card is finished, trim its edges. If your family has pinking shears (scissors that make a zigzag edge), you can use them to create an interesting effect. If you own a stamp set, you can stamp the word *postcard* on the back of the card. However, as long as you address

your card and stamp it, it will be delivered. These postcards are fun to make and send to friends.

The same card cut in two, lengthwise, is just the right size for a bookmark. They make attractive presents.

A box of stationery or notecards decorated with flowers pressed under contact paper makes a nice gift also. Cut a piece of contact paper large enough to leave a margin around the flower. This will leave enough paper around the edge to hold the flower firmly.

Drawing paper measuring twelve by eighteen inches is just the right size for making place mats. Design your mat on a clear sheet and then move the flowers and leaves to the contact paper. You can run the design around the outside in a border, or cover the entire sheet.

When you have finished laying the flowers on the plastic and gently pressing them with your fingers, start at the shorter edge and lay down the paper. Move it to the opposite end, smoothing it to make certain no wrinkles occur. If the paper wrinkles, lift it gently and smooth it out. Lining up the two sheets is sometimes tricky when you use such large sheets. When finished, trim the edges.

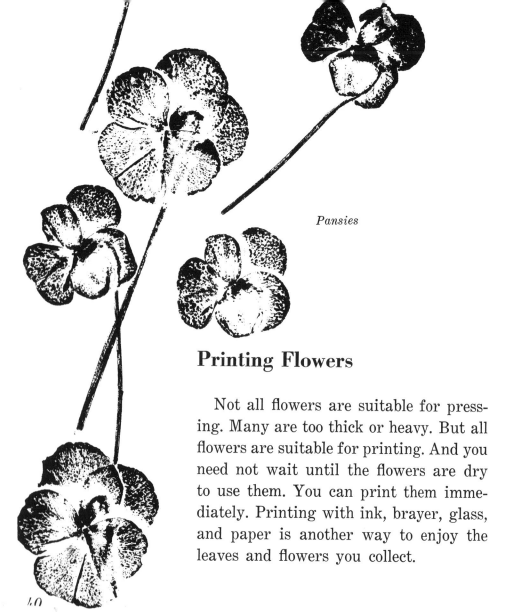

Pansies

Printing Flowers

Not all flowers are suitable for pressing. Many are too thick or heavy. But all flowers are suitable for printing. And you need not wait until the flowers are dry to use them. You can print them immediately. Printing with ink, brayer, glass, and paper is another way to enjoy the leaves and flowers you collect.

Holding the flower in your hand while printing it makes you more conscious of its stem, how the leaves are placed on it, and the size and shape of the flower itself. The print of a flower shows us a great deal about its structure. It helps us admire the plant for reasons other than its beauty.

Plants print better if they have not begun to wilt or dry out. If you cannot use them soon after picking, keep them immersed in water or wrapped in a wet paper towel.

Flower prints can be used on cards, notepaper, and place mats as well as for pictures.

Plants Found on the Sides of Roads

Buttercups have a single bright yellow flower with five petals. The leaves of the same plant often have different shapes. The petals spread in a horizontal circle, forming what is called a landing platform for bees and other insects. The flowers above it shine as though they were varnished. It may be this shiny reflection that shows up when you hold the buttercup under someone's chin. If the chin turns yellow it is said the person likes butter!

Buttercups belong to one of the oldest plant families.

Daisies have as many as twenty to thirty white petals. The petals are called banner flowers. The center is filled with yellow florets. Each one is a flower that produces a seed. Daisies are members of one of the newest flower families.

Butter-and-eggs are very pretty flowers which get their name from their two shades of yellow. One is lighter, like butter, and the other a deeper yellow like the yolk of an egg.

Fireweed grows along roadsides in many places. Its pink flowers are particu-

Vetch

Aster

larly plentiful in places where there has been a fire. Bees pollinate this tall plant, which often grows five feet tall. The silky seeds are enclosed in pods.

Queen Anne's lace got its name from a lace worn by Queen Anne of England. The lace was designed in circles much like those of the flower. The white blossom is umbrella-shaped, with a number of florets. A magnifying glass will show that each white floret has five petals with five tiny stamens. Queen Anne's lace also is called birds' nest, because of the way the floret's stems curl up and protect the ripening seeds. As many as 800 seeds have been counted on a single flower. This flower is beautiful when pressed.

Blue-eyed grass is often overlooked in the spring and early summer. You will see its dark blue six-petaled flower with a yellow center growing among the true grasses, which look like its own narrow leaves.

Hawkweeds have yellow, orange, or reddish flowers growing at the top of a hairy stem. The leaves grow in a circle on the ground at the base of the plant. You can find hawkweed leaves the year round. An ancient superstition says that hawks drank the juice of this plant to strengthen their keen eyesight!

Wild rose has five pink petals growing from a prickly stem. Roses belong to

the same family as apples and strawberries. Their fruit is red and is called a hip. The hip is edible and many people eat it because it is rich in vitamin C. You often see bees perched on the yellow stamens.

Vetch is a purple flower belonging to the pea family. It grows on a vine winding among other plants. The leaf has many separate leaflets with strings trailing from their tips. Seeds are contained in pods that are very much like the pods of peas we eat.

Aster means star in Latin. The star-shaped flowers bloom in many colors. There are about seventy kinds of asters in the United States. The flowers appear in the fall.

Goldenrod is the official flower of several states. There are about one hundred and twenty-five kinds of goldenrod growing in the United States. All of them are native to this country. You will see the flowers in the fall.

Milkweed is common along most roadsides. Many pinkish flowers grow on this tall plant. The flowers produce seeds that are protected in a large pod. When the pod bursts open the silky white seeds fly away on plumes. The plant gets its name from the sticky, milk-colored juice you see when it is broken or cut. The monarch butterfly visits the plant and deposits its eggs. The larvae feed on the large leaves.

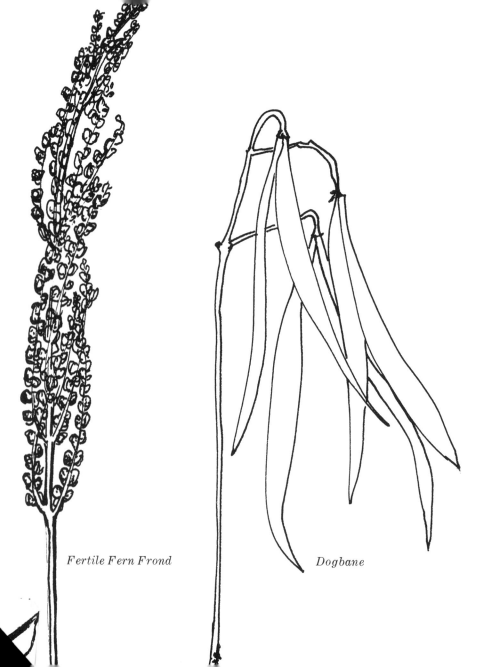

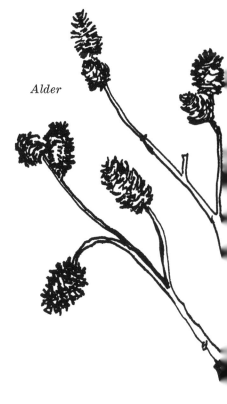

Alder

Fertile Fern Frond

Dogbane

Seed Pods

Seeds burst from the pods of milkweed and out of the tips of the cattail. They move through the air on tiny parachutes. Other seeds bristle with burrs that attach themselves to clothing or animal fur. Seeds find many ways to distribute themselves.

The fertilized seeds are mature. You cannot recognize the flower you once knew. The pretty blossom has turned into a ripe, dried, often oddly shaped container for seeds.

Rose seeds are held in bright red hips. The seeds of the wild pea, or vetch, are protected in a pod. Cockleburs, thistles, and burdocks protect and insure distribution of their seeds with hooked barbs and sharp points.

Fall plants and their seeds are often the subjects of dramatic photos. They find their way into homes in dried bouquets as reminders of summer days and examples of nature's beauty of design.

The variety of their shapes can be arranged artistically in countless ways. Alder cones, rose hips, vetch, and mustard pods, and the dried grasses timothy and redtop are common. The red berries of the sumac bush, the tall pointed spikes of the cattail, the split milkweed pods, and the dried sunflower heads add contrast to any collection. Cockleburs, burdocks, thistles, and the seed heads of caraway and asters are only a few of the plants that grow abundantly on the sides of roads.

The sharp outlines and intricate shapes of dried seed heads are excellent subjects for sun pictures.

Rose Hip

45

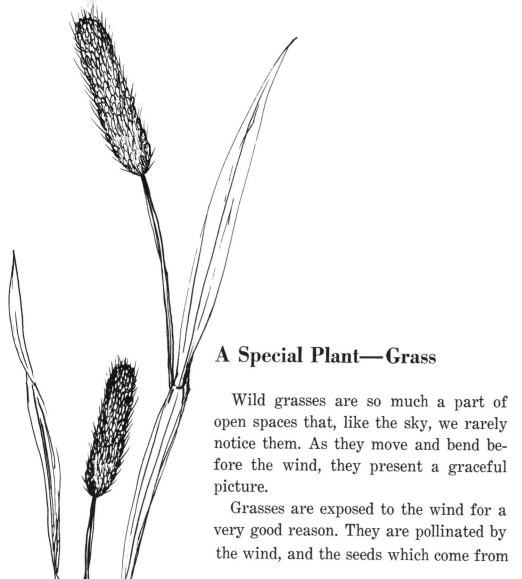

Meadow Foxtail

A Special Plant—Grass

Wild grasses are so much a part of open spaces that, like the sky, we rarely notice them. As they move and bend before the wind, they present a graceful picture.

Grasses are exposed to the wind for a very good reason. They are pollinated by the wind, and the seeds which come from the microscopic flowers are distributed by it. Of all plants, grasses have been the most useful to people. All the grains and cereals we eat are grass seeds.

We think of grasses as being alike. On looking closely we begin to notice that some have spikes, some have furry heads, others are feathery and branched. Wild barley, wild oats, timothy, redtop, quack grass, goose grass, panic grass, foxtail, and broom sedge are the names of a few common grasses.

Grasses are plentiful and a good material for many projects. Their long stems are graceful additions to bouquets. The seed heads make interesting sun pictures. They can be dried and glued into fall flower pictures. They are good subjects for printing, and finally, they are especially good subjects for nature weaving.

Brown Bent Grass

Red Top

Hair Grass

47

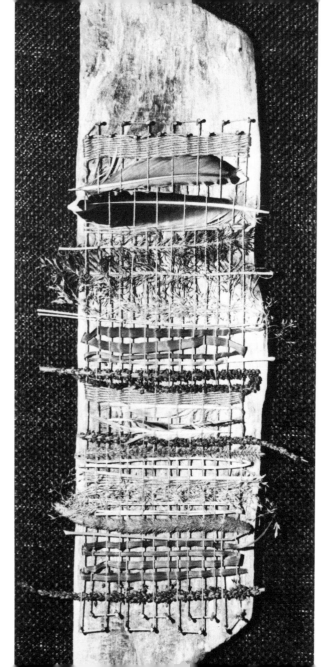

Weaving

Weaving is very simple. In the early days of civilization, people wove useful objects from natural materials.

Touching things is a special way of experiencing them. It is not a way we express ourselves very often. The roughness, the softness, the different lines and rhythms of objects that you can feel through your fingers and hands are very satisfying.

You can find a variety of things along the roadside to weave into patterns. Grasses of different kinds weave very well. They are tough yet supple. You will also find other natural objects which accent the grasses, like the soft gauzy texture of a bird's feather, a twig covered with lichen, or a dried seed pod. The woven pattern in the photo on page 48 combines several different textures. Collect many different objects for your weaving project.

Making a Loom

Weaving is done on a loom of some sort. The loom in the picture here is simply an old board with tiny nails tacked at both ends and strung with string. To make a loom then, you will need a board, nails, and some string or heavy thread.

You can arrange the nails across the loom in a straight line, or stagger them. They are easier to string if you line them up. Tack them firmly into the board.

Tie the string around a nail at a lower corner of the board. Run it up the board to the nail directly above it. Lead the string over to the next nail, and then down the board. Loop it around the nail at the bottom, then over to the next nail and up again.

Follow this pattern, pulling the string tightly, until you reach the last nail. Tie

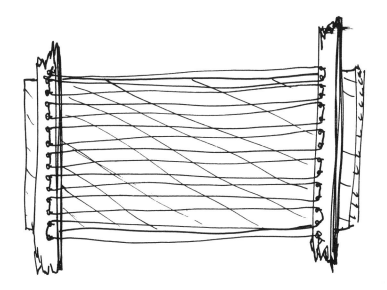

the string around the last nail to hold it in place. Once the loom is strung, you are ready to weave it with the grasses and other materials you have gathered.

Choose the grass with which you want to start. Move it over the first string, under the next, over and under, until you reach the opposite side. If the grass is long enough, fold it back and return it, over and under, to the starting point.

If you began your first row by pushing the stem over the first string and under the next, begin your second row in just the opposite way—push the stem of your grass or other plant under the first string and over the second. By alternating your weave, you will find that it holds together better; it will be a firmer fit. Continue alternating the rows until you reach the bottom of your loom.

The hanging reproduced in the photo has patterns. Some of the materials are repeated many times, like the chorus of a song. Others, such as the feather, are used as an accent. Some of the thread that was used in stringing the loom was woven in to add a contrasting color. Other pieces of string or yarn can be woven in, too.

As you add more materials and different patterns your weaving will take on a life of its own. It will become a pleasing object to hang on your wall. It will express to your friends your eye for design and your special sense of touch.

3

yards and gardens

Insect Watchers

Everybody has seen bird watchers. They carry binoculars, make long lists of the birds they have found, and often travel long distances to see new and different birds. We have all heard of bird watchers, but what about insect watchers?

Insect watchers are a quiet group. They rarely go beyond their own yard. There is so much to watch there. They don't use binoculars, though sometimes they spend hours watching insects of all kinds.

What do they see? They almost always see honeybees visiting flowers to collect pollen. They watch ladybird beetles attack aphids on infested plants. They watch ants go in and out of their hills and try to make some sense of their movement.

They catch fireflies and hold them captive on a summer's night. And they marvel at the beauty of each butterfly that flutters across the lawn.

From their very doorstep the insect watchers can observe the complex markings on the broad, strong wings of butterflies. They can watch the weak-winged but strong-legged grasshoppers leap long distances and see their mouths move from side to side (not up and down) as they chew their way through a leafy meal.

The compound, many-lensed insect eyes may lead the watchers to think about the world as it is seen by insects. The feathery antennae of moths will prompt them to find out how this special instrument for feeling is used. And most of all they will see how an insect's outside skeleton, which is always divided into three parts and supported by three pairs of legs, changes dramatically as it moves through its life cycle.

Insects are short-lived. In most cases there is a new generation each year. All insect lives, like those of flowers, are organized and directed toward producing new generations. Insects assure their survival by growing to adulthood in stages.

Female insects deposit eggs through an organ called an ovipositor. They lay their eggs on leaves, or under rocks, or inside the barks of trees. In each egg, as in the seeds of plants, is a tiny living thing. Each of these living things will grow and, like its parents, reproduce itself.

Some insects, such as grasshoppers, hatch fully formed from eggs, looking like tiny adults. They grow by gradual stages into adults, just as we do. Other insects, such as butterflies, hatch from the eggs as caterpillars. Their job is to eat and grow.

The caterpillar feeds on leaves, shedding its skin whenever it outgrows the old one. When it is fully grown, it stops eating. But it is not yet an adult. First it must build a cocoon for itself. It sometimes remains in the cocoon all winter. Inside it changes its form. Insect watchers tell us how exciting it is to be there when the insect emerges from its cocoon, the caterpillar now transformed into a gorgeous butterfly.

With such sights waiting for us, it is hard to resist becoming a backyard insect watcher. As you watch the many different kinds of insects, you may want to keep a permanent record by making large, colorful models of your favorites.

Strip-Mache Insects

Look at an insect closely. Any insect— a bee, a caterpillar, a butterfly, or a ladybird beetle. How large are its wings? Where are they attached to its body? How long are its legs? Are they strong, or are they small and not very apparent?

Every insect's body is composed of three parts, a head, a thorax, and an abdomen. What is the size of its head in relation to the other parts of its body? Once you have a clear impression of the insect, you are ready to build a strip-mache insect of your own.

Buy a package of art tissue paper in an art supply store. It comes in a package of many colors. This paper will become your insect's outer covering. Also buy a small bag of wallpaper paste in a hardware store. Collect a pile of old newspapers, a large brown grocery bag, and eight short lengths of wire.

Tear some of the newspapers into two-inch strips and lay them on your work table. Mix the wallpaper paste in a bowl with water until it becomes soupy. Do not let the paste mixture get too thin. Crumple the rest of the newspapers into balls.

Stuff the brown paper bag with the balls of newspaper. Tie a string around the bag's opening to keep the papers from falling out. This forms the body of your insect. Divide the insect into its three parts by tying two more strings tightly around it. One string marks off the head from the thorax, and the other marks off the thorax from the abdomen.

Dip a newspaper strip into the paste. Run the strip through your fingers, dripping the excess paste back into the bowl. Wrap the strip around the paper bag. Take another strip, and another, pasting them first in one direction, then in another, until you have covered the entire surface of the bag.

Then paste on a second layer of strips. This layer helps to make the body of your insect firm. Again, run the strips in many different directions, covering the entire body. Let the pasted strips dry.

Now make the other parts of the insect. Form its wings with about three sheets of newspaper, folding them to get the shape you want. Cover them with pasted strips. Stick them on the insect's body with other pasted strips.

Use six short pieces of wire for the legs. Wrap the wire in newspaper to the desired thickness. You can bend them to get the shape you want, while the wire inside keeps them firm. Cover the wire and newspaper with pasted strips. When you are attaching the legs, put several layers of paper strips on the insect's underside, then wind them around the top part of the legs before pasting them down. This step holds the legs securely to the body.

Make the antennae the same way. Wrap newspaper around your two remaining wires. Bend them to look like antennae. Cover them with pasted strips of paper. Then fasten them to the head with other pasted strips.

At this point look over your insect carefully. Paste more strips wherever they are needed to cover and strenghten it.

Now you are ready to add your insect's colorful skin. Plan your pattern of colors before cutting the colored tissue into strips. What color do you want the wings, legs, and body? Spots, stripes, and other patterns can be added to the insect by cutting them from the tissue.

Cut the paper into strips. Do not dip them into the paste because they will lose their bright colors. Brush the paste carefully onto the colored tissue strips, and then add two or three layers of them over the insect's body. The brilliant colors will bring your insect alive.

Set the completed insect aside overnight. The pasted strips dry into a hard covering of great strength.

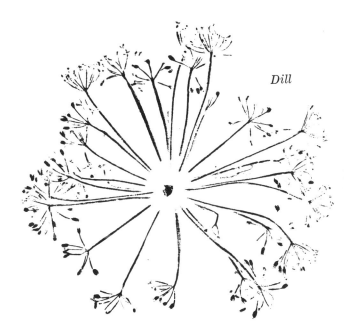

Dill

Bees, Flowers, and Colors

Yards contain gardens in which flowers and vegetables grow. We plant the flowers because they are pretty. They add color to the summer days. When we have flowers, we will have bees, too, for all the flowers will be pollinated by some visiting insect.

Butterflies pollinate some flowers, mainly those that are orange or red. Moths pollinate flowers such as honeysuckle that open their fragrant blossoms at night. But most flowers are pollinated by families of bees which search for pollen and nectar to support their hives.

Their hairy abdomens and legs and their fuzzy bodies make bees perfect partners for the blue and yellow flowers to which their eyes are sensitive. They visit thousands each season, storing the pollen in a special structure on their back legs. Then they carry the pollen to their hives. Sometimes they travel as much as a mile, their honey baskets laden with pollen.

Colorful flowers and their fragrances are a part of our enjoyment of a garden. But the bees, drawn there by the colors, are also a reward for growing a garden.

Light Window Pictures

Flowers from blossoming trees or culti-vated gardens are colorful, and often larger than wild flowers. They have been bred to produce these showy flowers. Press cultivated flowers as you would wild ones (see Part II). You can use them in much the same way for stationery, notecards, bookmarks, and place mats. But these splendid flowers are particularly effective in light window pictures.

How to Make Light Window Pictures

Light shining through a plant vividly reveals the structure of the flower and the leaves. Mounting plants to hang in

windows as light pictures is a good way to study their structure.

To make light window pictures, you need contact paper, colored construction paper, scissors, paste, string, and your pressed flowers and leaves. You also need a special paper called rice paper which you can buy in an art supply store.

The size of your light picture will depend on the size of the flowers and leaves you have collected. Cut the contact paper and the rice paper to the proper size for the finished picture. Six inches by ten inches should be about right, though you might want to vary it a little.

Lay the flowers and the leaves down on the contact paper. Keep a margin of about an inch around the edge of the contact paper. This will give you space to add a frame. Lay the rice paper over the flowers

Dogwood

and contact paper. Press with your fingers around flowers and leaves.

Select two sheets of construction paper. With a ruler and pencil, make a margin on each sheet an inch from the edge on all sides. Cut out the part inside the margin. Now you have a frame. Glue a frame to each side of the light picture. Put a thread through a tiny hole at the top and hang your picture in a window.

Ladybird Beetle

Little Black Ant

Bumblebee

Some Common Insects Found in the Yard and Garden

Grasshopper is a good example of camouflage. Its green body is almost invisible in the grass. Grasshoppers have long thighs with strong muscles that allow them to jump great distances. Their jaws are shaped for biting and grinding leaves. Nymphs emerge in the spring from eggs that are laid in the ground the previous fall.

Spittlebugs are named for the froth the females leave on stems to conceal their eggs. Nymphs leave this froth or spittle on stems, too. If you look into it you may find a small greenish spittlebug feeding there.

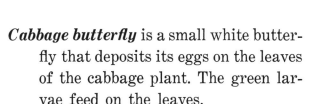

Cabbage butterfly is a small white butterfly that deposits its eggs on the leaves of the cabbage plant. The green larvae feed on the leaves.

Ladybird beetles often lay their eggs on plants infested with aphids. Both the adults and the larvae feed on these harmful insects. Ladybird beetles are red with black spots.

Cecropia moth is a large, beautiful insect which pollinates flowers at night. Its wings are often six inches across. In winter it attaches its large cocoon to a tree.

Bumblebees have hairy bodies which carry pollen from plant to plant. The large mouth parts of bumblebees can reach into plants such as red clover which are too deep for other insects.

Fireflies are soft-bodied beetles. The female, sometimes wingless, is called a glowworm. A segment in the abdomen contains light-producing tissue.

Insect galls are swollen parts of plant tissue where insects have laid their eggs. As the eggs hatch, the plant around the larvae begins to swell. The larvae feed on plant juices.

Isabella moth, yellowish with black spots, is first seen in late May. Woolly bears are the furry, black-and-red banded caterpillars of the Isabella moth. The caterpillar feeds on grasses and garden plants and does not make a cocoon until spring.

Ants work together to gather food and care for the nest. The constant going and coming of these insects is good for the soil, allowing air to enter it. The larvae of ants, white capsules like rice grains, are often found under rocks.

Cabbage Butterfly

Woolly Bear

Beet

Parts of a Vegetable

All plants have roots, stems, flowers, and fruits. The plant works hard to make food during its growing season. But vegetables make more food than they can use. They store it in various other places as well as in their seeds. They can store it in their leaves, roots, bulbs, or fruits.

We cultivate certain plants for the food they store and harvest them for our own nourishment. We eat the seeds of peas, beans, sunflowers, and corn. We eat the roots of carrots, beets, and turnips, and the tubers or nodules of potatoes. We eat the leaves of lettuce and spinach and the fruits of squash, cucumbers, tomatoes, and peppers.

Gardens and the vegetable section of the supermarket are filled with interesting plant stories. Each part of the plant we eat played a part in the plant's history.

Leaves

Leaves are the food factories of flowering plants. Leaves capture sunlight and make food from the carbon dioxide of the air and the water and minerals taken from the earth by the plant's roots.

Vegetable counters are filled with a variety of leafy vegetables for sale. Here is a project to help you watch some roots and bulbs grow into leaves during the winter months. You can watch these vegetables create their own food factories.

Leaf Garden

Bulbs and root vegetables will grow leaves from their tops in a dish garden in your home. As long as they have moisture and light the roots and bulbs will continue to grow. They will provide you with a bit of green and a chance to watch growing things in the winter.

Fill a low dish with gravel or pebbles. Carrots, beets, turnips, parsnips, and on-

Onion

Carrot

ions can all grow in dish gardens. Cut away any leaves from the vegetable's top and set it in the gravel dish. Cut the carrot about two inches below the top to fit into the low dish. Arrange your vegetables so they are firmly settled in the pebbles, add some water, and place the dish in a sunny window.

Check this dish garden daily to watch its progress and see that it remains moist. Each day you will notice some new growth. In about ten days you will have a flourishing leaf garden.

Roots

Leaves always grow up toward the light. Roots grow down into the soil, prob-

ing for water and nourishing minerals. They keep the plant anchored in place.

Because roots most often stay underground, we are not usually aware of them. But all of us are familiar with the roots of certain plants such as carrots, beets, and radishes because the root is the part of those plants which we eat.

Because roots are thick and firm, they can hold ink and their shapes can be printed just as those of leaves and flowers.

Stamp Printing with Vegetables

Many interesting patterns can be stamped from vegetables. They create a very personal wrapping paper, interesting place mats, and border decorations for notepaper.

Any firm root vegetable makes a good stamp. Carrots, red beets, parsnips, and potatoes can be cut and stamped on paper. You can cut various designs into the vegetable, such as stars, bars, or petals.

Paper, ink, a pane of glass, a brayer, a paring knife, and vegetables are the only materials you need. Stamps can be cut from the vegetables in two ways, making two kinds of designs.

Slice a root vegetable so that its end is smooth and clean. If you cut away most of the surface, leaving only your design, you will have a true stamp in a raised design. If you cut your design into the vegetable's flat surface, you will get an entirely different effect. The vegetable's

surface will then enclose your design.

Roll some ink onto the glass with your brayer. When the ink sounds sticky, press the end of the vegetable with your design into the ink. Stamp the mat, card, or tissue you want to decorate. Sometimes you can stamp several times before inking the vegetable again. Use different colored inks to create additional interest.

Seeds

We have seen that the life of a plant moves purposefully toward the goal of seed production. We have watched trees, weeds, wild flowers, and vegetables grow green leaves, mature flowers, and produce seeds in the city, along roadsides, and in our backyards. It is interesting to lay out before us the varieties of seeds and observe their differences and to think about the lives they will lead when they are planted.

Vegetable plants, grown for their nourishing seeds, provide us with seeds far larger than those we normally find in wild plants. Each seed contains a new plant, along with the nutrition it needs. Cut one open and look at the tiny curled-up plant inside. It is ready to start its life cycle as a plant and finally produce seeds of its own.

Seed Mosaics

It is possible to look at seeds in another way. To look at them for their color, shape, size, and texture is to think of them artistically. You can use seeds to create a design or an interesting picture.

Some artists create pictures from tiny pieces of glass or tile, building up patterns that are called mosaics. That is what you can do with seeds. You need seeds, El-

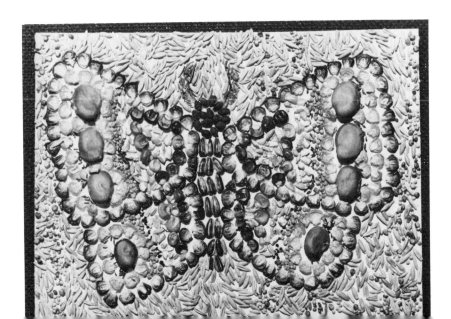

mer's glue, and a stiff background—mat board or a stiff cardboard will do. Collect as many kinds of seeds as you can find, outdoors, in the kitchen, and from the bird feeder. Beans, peas, sunflowers, maple seeds are a few you can find and use to make a mosaic.

Sketch in a design or picture, keeping in mind the different kinds of seeds you have to use. Now begin to create patterns on the background, gluing in areas of one kind of seed and then another. If you are making a flower, you might form the stem from one kind of seed, the petals from another, the leaves from yet another. Spread the glue in one area, lay down the seeds, and then move to another area. When you are finished, lay aside the mosaic to dry.

Corn Husk Dolls

An ear of corn is protected by a casing called a husk. A husk is a kind of leaf that has many uses. Early settlers used corn husks to fashion dolls for their children. In those households where objects made from anything other than natural materials were very rare, corn husk dolls were welcome toys.

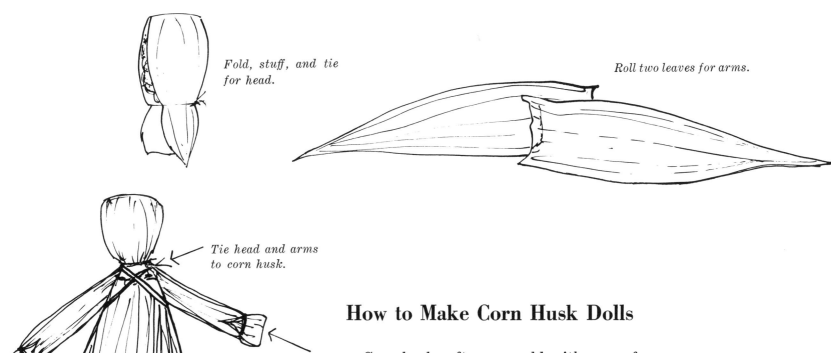

*Fold, stuff, and tie
for head.*

Roll two leaves for arms.

*Tie head and arms
to corn husk.*

*Fold back and tie
for hands.*

How to Make Corn Husk Dolls

Corn husks often are sold with ears of decorative corn in the fall. They also remain on the corn sold at grocery counters. A pan of water, a corn husk, some single leaves from corn husks, string, and an empty soda bottle are the only materials you need.

For the doll's body choose a full husk with a stem on it. Set this husk over an

empty soda bottle, with its stem pointing up. Tie some string around the part of the husk which will be the doll's waist, about an inch and a half or two inches below the stem.

Have several other single leaves soaking in the pan of water. Soaked leaves are easy to bend and tie. Take two of the wet leaves, roll them, and bend them forward over the shoulders to make the arms. Hold them firmly in place while tying with the string, first forward and then backward in the form of a cross on both the front and back of the body.

When the arms are firmly lashed to the body, turn up their bottom edges to form the hands. Tie at the wrist with another strip of wet corn husk.

Make a head by pulling together some scraps and covering them with a larger piece of husk. Squeeze and pull into shape and set the head over the husk's stem. Tie it lightly with a string. If the stem is too long, trim it. Cover the string with strips of husk and tie in back.

For a shawl, cut a long leaf halfway down the center. Slip this piece over the head and bring the two ends to the front, crossing them over each other. Tie another strip around the middle of the shawl. An apron can be cut to size from another leaf and a belt tied around the waist.

Corn silk makes attractive hair. Cut a hat from the base of the leaf, then cup it around the head and trim it. Use pins to fasten the hat. Tie another strip under the chin for bonnet strings.

4

the forest

Pine Needle

The Forest

During the Middle Ages forest trees were sometimes thought to be inhabited by spirits. The ancient priests in England, called Druids, worshipped trees and other forest plants. There was an old belief that if the spores, or fruiting bodies, of a certain kind of fern fell on a person's napkin, the person would become invisible. Fairies and elves were said to have danced on the tops of umbrella-shaped mushrooms and gathered beneath them at night for riotous parties.

The forest was a place of magic and mystery to our ancestors. Apparently

Meadow Rue

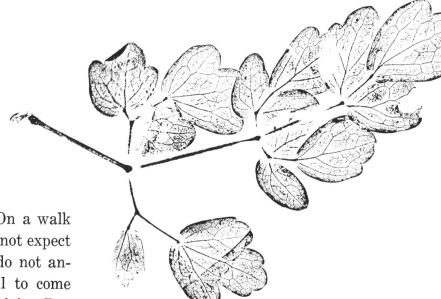

anything could happen there. On a walk through the forest today we do not expect to be made invisible, and we do not anticipate at a bend in the trail to come upon a convention of elves or fairies. But for modern people the forest may be a kind of magical place, too.

The emerald green of damp, moss-covered rocks that reflect an eerie light falling through a thick canopy of leaves makes us feel as if we are in another world. And, in a sense, we are. All around us, at the base of the dark tree trunks, are the curious shapes of cones, ferns, and mushrooms. They remind us that we have entered a primeval world—one that existed long before people or the other animals we know were on earth. This wealth of forms was not created for our entertainment but to insure the reproduction of these prehistoric plants.

Mushrooms emerging from the forest floor in moist dark spots are the fruiting bodies of long underground threads called a mycelium. Lichens are two plants in one. They are composed of an alga and a fungus. They reproduce by means of spores that drift away on the wind to other places.

The green mosses contain spores in capsules held on a stalk high above the tiny two-inch plants. The reproductive cycle of ferns requires four stages to transform the tiny spores into new plants.

None of these plants has flowers as we know them. They are, in fact, called nonflowering plants, and together they comprise a large part of the world's growing organisms.

Many of these plants can be gathered easily. You can create your own model of the forest floor.

How to Make a Terrarium

When you are on an outing to the woods, gather a variety of woodland plants. Mosses and lichens, a small fern, a tiny sapling, or plants whose leaves stay green all winter, such as checkerberry, cranberry, or partridgeberry, all make good terrarium plants. Place them carefully in a container with some soil around them so they will not dry out. A little water in the container or some moist paper towels will keep the plants damp and fresh.

The best container for your garden or terrarium is a deep glass bowl or aquar-

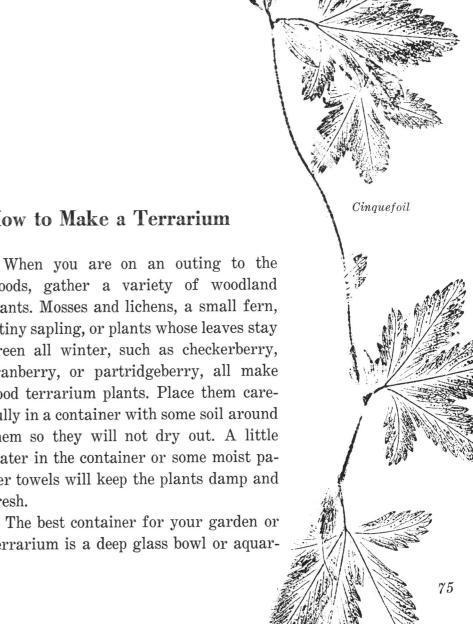

Cinquefoil

75

ium. The glass container will allow you to see your plants easily. If it is deep enough, it will allow your plants to fit comfortably beneath a cover or lid.

Find some pebbles, sand or gravel, charcoal, and soil as a base for your plants. Pebbles in the bottom of the container will provide good drainage. Over the pebbles pour a layer of sand and a layer of ground charcoal. You can buy ground charcoal at a florist shop, but flattened barbecue briquettes can also be used. The top level consists of one or two inches of top soil, depending on the size and depth of your container.

Arrange all of your plants in the container in a little forest scene. As you

work, keep turning the container so that you see it from all sides. A moss-covered rock or a lichen-covered branch often adds interest to the plants and makes the scene appear more like a forest. After arranging all the material, water it lightly and put a sheet of glass or plastic over the top of the container.

Move your terrarium to a window that is not sunny. Too much sun will cause the plants to dry out and turn brown. If droplets of water collect on the sides or the top of your terrarium, remove the lid. Exposure to the air for a few hours will allow the moisture to escape. Water the terrarium occasionally. Your garden will remain fresh looking all winter.

Mushrooms

The white threads of mushrooms are hidden underground. This plant, which

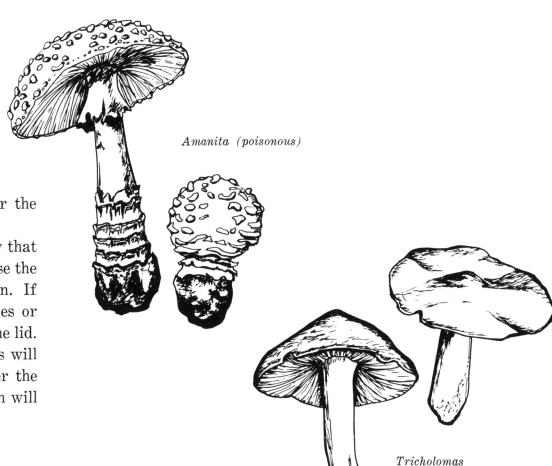

Amanita (poisonous)

Tricholomas

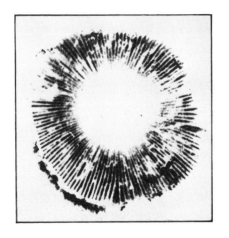

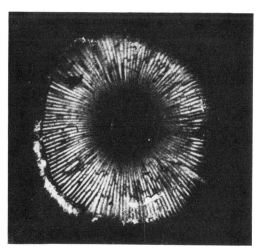

number of shapes. They can be concave, convex, depressed, raised, or shaped like a funnel. But whatever its shape, a mushroom's job is to send out hundreds of tiny fertile bodies called spores. Like the seeds of flowers, spores are a mushroom's way of making a new generation.

Mushrooms carry their spores on their undersides. Many have plates or gills among which the spores are lodged. You can capture the spores of these mushrooms on paper and make a kind of print.

How to Make a Spore Print

Choose a fresh mushroom with a flat cap. An old dried mushroom will have already dropped its spores. Cut off the stem close to the cap. Put the cap flat on

lacks chlorophyll, lives on food taken by its threads from the cells of dead wood and from soil enriched by dead leaves. Decay is all about you in some stage in the forest. It is the process by which mushrooms and other fungi break down dead materials and turn them into nourishment for themselves.

Rising so mysteriously from the leaves of the forest floor, mushrooms can have a

Cinnamon Fern

a sheet of paper. Cover the cap with a jar for three or four hours. Remove the jar and the cap carefully.

You will find the spores have dropped into a fascinating design on the paper. Each species of mushroom makes a design of its own. Some spores are white, others are brown. If you use colored paper you will get an interesting contrast in your spore print. Spray the finished print with a fixative so that it will not smear. You can buy fixative at a hobby shop.

Ferns

Ferns growing along forest trails are remnants of entire forests of fern trees which grew ages ago. In fact, those fos-

Cinnamon Fern

Interrupted Fern

Cedar

silized forests make up what are now most of our coal deposits.

The long green leaves of ferns grow from an underground stem. Each year from the end of that stem several beautiful fronds emerge. If you look at the base of the stem where it comes from the ground, you can see the remains of last year's leaves.

During early spring, lightly curled buds, covered with woolly scales, will appear in the woods. These are fiddleheads, or young ferns. Slowly the buds will uncurl. In some of the larger ferns they will grow as much as five feet high.

The fruiting bodies of a fern often grow on the back of its leaves. They too are called spores. They are carried in a case which creates a pattern on each leaf-

let or pinnule. The case protects the spores. By its characteristic pattern it helps us to identify the fern.

Ferns are among the loveliest objects in nature. It would be hard to decide which among the thousands of kinds are the most beautiful. Ferns make excellent subjects for both drying and printing.

Interrupted Fern

Nonflowering Trees

Pine, spruce, larch, fir, hemlock, juniper, cedar, and redwoods are groups of nonflowering trees that grow throughout our country. Most of these trees are evergreen. Nearly all bear cones.

The cones, seeds, and needlelike leaves of these trees also make excellent subjects for nature plaques. Parts of these ancient trees, embedded in plastic remind us of the fossilized remains of their ancestors.

How to Make Tree Plaques

Buy a small container of plaster of Paris at a hardware store. If you do not have some clay or plasteline at home, you

Tree Plaque of Maple Leaf and Seed Pod

Cedar

can buy it at an art supply store. Collect the materials for your plaque. The tips of evergreen branches and their cones make clear, pleasing designs.

Roll out the clay or plasteline as you would a pie crust, until you have a smooth surface nearly three-fourths of an inch thick. Using additional clay, make a wall an inch high around the rim so that you now have a small clay pot in which to hold the plaster of Paris.

Mix the plaster of Paris in a bowl, following the instructions on the side of the box. Select the leaves and cones you wish to use. Cones, the needlelike leaves, and seeds, all chosen from the same tree, reveal something about the life of that tree. Gently but firmly press them into the clay. Lift the pieces gently. You now have a print of the tree parts in the clay.

Pour the plaster of Paris into the mold you have made. Set it aside for twenty-four hours, until it is completely dry. By that time the plaster will have hardened into a plaque. Peel the clay away from the plaque.

What was depressed in the clay is now raised on the plaster, and you have an impression of the tree. Dry tempera paint, available in any art supply store, can be rubbed over the face of the plaque to give it a finished look. Buy an adhesive picture hook at a ten-cent store and fix it to the back of the plaque, or carefully drill a hole through the plaque for hanging.

Make several plaques, using material from a different tree on each. One cedar plaque, for instance, one of pine, and another of spruce will give you variety. Groups of these plaques hung on a wall make an attractive exhibition. The fruits and blossoms of hardwood trees, such as oaks and maples, also make good plaques.

Never dispose of your leftover plaster of Paris by pouring it down the sink or the toilet. It will plug up the pipes.

Pyxie Cups

Some Nonflowering Plants Found in the Woods

FUNGI

Mushrooms are the umbrella-shaped fruiting organs of threads which live on dead vegetation. Without fungi the forest would be choked with dead materials. They reproduce by spores that fall from the caps and throw out threads. There are many kinds of mushrooms with different colors and shapes.

Tree fungi are also called bracket fungi or shelf mushrooms because they grow from the trunk of a tree. The spores of a fungus are blown into cuts or wounds on trees and the new fungus lives off the tree. You often see these fungi growing on dead trees. You can draw pictures on their hard, flat undersurface.

LICHENS

Boulder lichens are found on rocks or on old wood. A lichen is really two plants living together, a fungus and an alga. They help to make soil.

Reindeer lichens are said to resemble the antlers of the reindeer, which uses it for food.

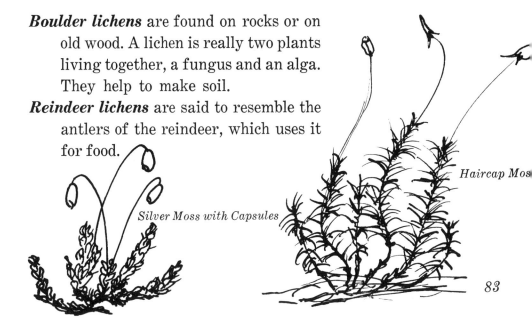

Haircap Moss

Silver Moss with Capsules

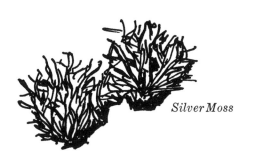

Silver Moss

Cushion Moss

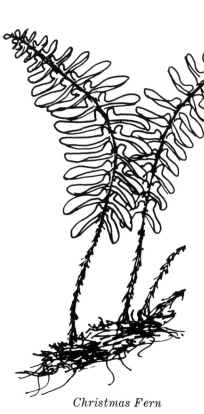

Christmas Fern

Pyxie cup is another kind of lichen. It is pale green. It gets its name because its tiny head is in the shape of a cup. Its strange shape makes it an interesting terrarium plant.

MOSSES

Haircap moss, like other mosses, grows from spores produced in capsules. The capsule of this moss is at the tip of a long stalk. The top of the capsule is hairy.

Sphagnum is a peat moss. It is often sold in florist shops and used to help young plants grow. It will hold a lot of moisture.

FERNS

Bracken, like all ferns, grows from an underground stem. The long green fronds we see each year are the growing tips. Bracken has a triangular leaf. This fern grows all over the world.

Sensitive fern is a large green fern that is sensitive to cold weather and is

British Soldiers

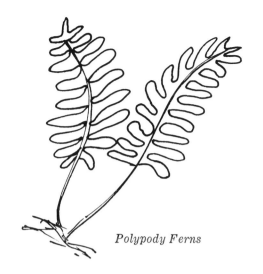

Polypody Ferns

easily killed by frost. It wilts quickly after picking. The spores of this fern are carried on a separate stem.

Christmas fern, which remains green all winter, carries its spores on the back of the leaflets. This fern gets its name because each part of the leaflet or pinnule is said to have the shape of a Christmas stocking. It is also one of the few ferns still green in the northern United States at Christmas time.

Reindeer Lichen

here are some more ways to use natural materials in holiday decorations.

Gift Wrappings

Printing plain tissue paper of various colors with pine, cedar, or fir makes a seasonal wrap. Try combining some of the boughs, mixing them in your print to create interesting patterns.

Christmas Decorations

Gift Tags

At Christmas we bring the forest indoors. The Christmas tree spreads the aroma of the forest through our homes and brightens our holiday. Evergreen boughs, made into sprays and wreaths, are a part of Christmas, too. Pictured

Press leaves or other natural materials gathered from the woods as you did earlier (see page 38). Cut to the proper size some plain index cards, oak tag, or stiff paper. There are a variety of sizes and shapes shown in the photo. Cut a piece of contact paper the same size. Lay the dried wood material on the card and cover it with the contact paper. Trim the edges. These tags were trimmed with pinking shears, but any scissors will do. Punch a hole at the top of the tag with a paper puncher and run a string through it. Write your message on the back and tie it to the package.

Gift Sprays

Some of us like to put a lot of care and attention into wrapping gifts. It is a good way to give two gifts at one time. For instance, the floral spray used to decorate the wrapping on a gift box can become a corsage once the package has been opened.

Cones, evergreen sprays, rose hips, dried grasses, or clumps of lichen can all go into the gift spray you plan to make. Buy a package of florist wires at a ten-cent store or florist shop. Lay out on the table your material from the woods, the wires, and some ribbon.

It helps to arrange all the pieces into a design before wiring them, just to make certain you are satisfied with it. Then begin fastening your spray together. Choose a large flat evergreen twig as the

base of the spray. Choose a piece for the next layer, wrap a wire around it and attach it to an end of your base twig. Keep adding material, fastening each piece to a part of the layer below it. When all your material is wired together in a spray, tie a ribbon around it. Fix the bow over the wire. The bow hides the wire and adds a final decoration to the spray.

Cards and Place Mats

Special cards and place mats can be printed for the holiday season. Use cuttings from evergreen branches, ferns, or other evergreen plants such as checkerberry or partridgeberry. The instructions for making cards and place mats are in Part II. These items make attractive Christmas gifts.

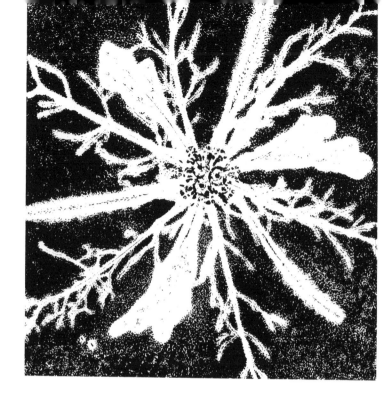

Christmas Stars

Cones, grasses, evergreen boughs, dried seed heads, rose hips, mosses, and lichens are a few of the natural materials that can be used to make this lovely Christmas decoration.

Lay out your materials, scissors, Duco cement, and a spool of thread. Cut two circles, one to one-and-a-half inches in diameter, from cardboard, birch bark, or other stiff material.

Cover one circle with Duco cement. Lay pine needles, stems of dried grass, or other long flat objects around the circle, so they radiate from the center, forming a star. Before gluing the second circle on top of the first, cut a length of thread and place it between the circles. This provides a string with which to hang the decoration. Press the circles firmly together.

The individual scales of pine cones, tiny scraps of cedar or spruce, dried seeds, rose hips, or other small parts of plants are added one by one to the outside of one circle. Cover the glued circle with them. You will begin to notice the beauty and variety of these tiny parts of plants in a way you never did before. Allow the star to dry for a few hours before decorating the opposite side. When you turn over the star to work on the opposite side, set it on a roll of tape or some other object that will raise the completed side from the surface of the table. It will be easier to work on the second side if it is raised. These Christmas stars made from natural materials can be hung in windows, over mantels and doorways, and on Christmas trees.

Wild Flowers

For a brief time in the spring, before the trees put forth their leaves, you will find a marvelous variety of wild flowers on the forest floor. Their blossoms push

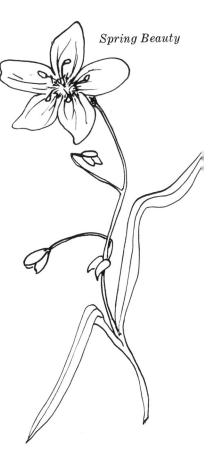

Spring Beauty

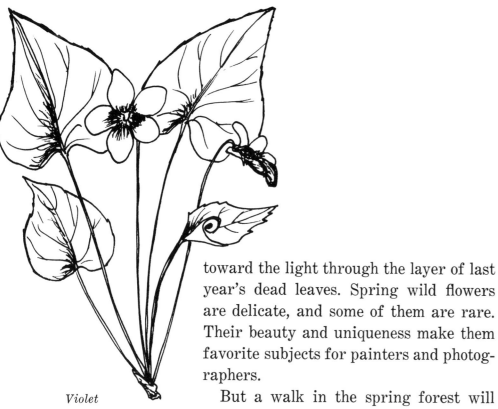

Violet

toward the light through the layer of last year's dead leaves. Spring wild flowers are delicate, and some of them are rare. Their beauty and uniqueness make them favorite subjects for painters and photographers.

But a walk in the spring forest will certainly show you some of these isolated flowers. If you see the dramatic shape of a lady's slipper, a jack-in-the-pulpit, Virginia bluebells, or Dutchman's-breeches, you will never forget them. Look for their pictures and their names in a guidebook to wild flowers. Learn to recognize them and call them by name. And then leave the flowers for the next walker to enjoy. A single flower and a single person in the forest together create a special moment.

Violets are among the few wild flowers that grow plentifully in the forest. Most forest flowers produce few seeds, but the violets have a special way of producing seeds to insure their abundance. You often see whole patches of blue violets. A few can be picked and pressed without endangering them.

But many of the forest wild flowers are fighting for existence. So much of the land on which they grow has been taken for buildings and roads that the living space they need shrinks every year. The best way to enjoy wild flowers is to go and look at them in the places where they grow.

5

the shore

Driftwood Mobile

92

Printed Driftwood

Shores

There are several kinds of shores, but nearly all of them are of rock. It is the size of the rock particles that makes the difference. Rock breaks down into boulders, pebbles, sand, or mud.

Rocky shores draped with seaweeds provide homes for mussels, barnacles, snails, sea urchins, and starfish, clinging among the ledges. Shores strewn with pebbles or boulders give little shelter for living things. Sandy shores hide worms, moon shells, and clams beneath their surface. Muddy shores, protected from the full force of storm waves, have rich stands of sea plants.

The picture here is of a printing of weathered driftwood. Parts of old trees, boats, crates, or wharves drift on the sea. They are washed in salt water and pounded by wind-driven waves on rocky and sandy shores.

Look for driftwood along the shore. Its shape broken and twisted, its interior pitted with insect holes, and its surface grooved and smoothed by salt, sand, and wind, driftwood becomes a reflection of nature's harsh forces. It tells us something about life on the open beaches.

Printing Driftwood

Lay the wood out in front of you. Look at its grain, which is the pattern made by its tissues. Run your fingers lightly over the markings left on the once living wood by water and weather. What you see and feel now, you will record in your driftwood print.

Assemble your brayer, ink, a pane of glass, paper, and the pieces of driftwood you have chosen to print.

Ink the glass with the brayer. The ink is the right consistency when the glass begins to sound sticky. Run the inked brayer back and forth over the surface of a piece of driftwood, making certain that it is thoroughly inked.

Lay the printing paper on top of the wood. Run your hand firmly over it. With your fingertips, follow the grain of the wood beneath the paper, as you felt for the fish scales and leaf veins in your earlier prints. Pressing the paper into all of

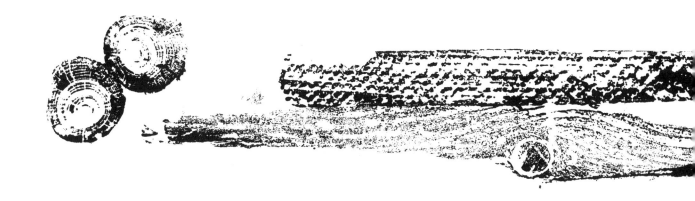

the wood's hollows and patterns enables you to transfer its variety to your paper.

Take several prints of the same piece of wood. Each will be different from the previous one because of the varying amounts of ink on the wood. Or make prints of several pieces of wood on the same paper, contrasting their textures. Mount your favorite prints on construction paper or mat board.

Driftwood Sculptures

Driftwood is often collected by dealers, who sell it to crafts people. The crafts people make lamp bases and other useful objects from the wood. Molded and decorated by nature—sand, wind, and salt water—this wood is pleasing to work with and display for others to admire.

On a visit to the beach you may find a

piece of driftwood you would like to keep. Take it home and make a driftwood sculpture.

Nature, of course, has already sculptured it for you. All you have to do is display it. Look over your piece of driftwood. Turn it this way and that, finding the position in which it looks best. Then choose a flattened piece of driftwood for a base. Hammer a small nail through the bottom of the base into the driftwood to anchor it in place. You can also apply Elmer's glue for added strength.

Your mounted driftwood sculpture makes an attractive ornament for a bookshelf or desk.

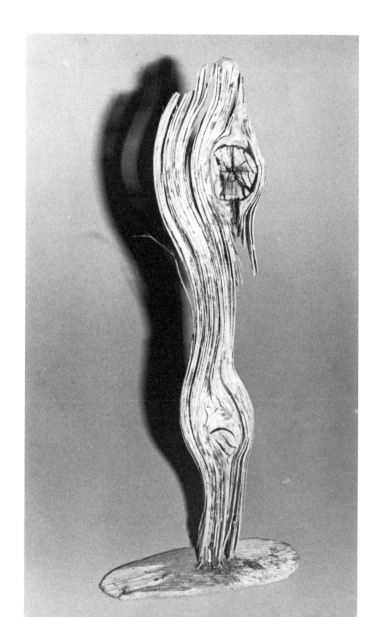

How to Make a Mobile

In making a mobile you will see once more the driftwood's grain and the complex rhythms that the sea and weather have worn into its surface.

Collect screw eyes, thread or nylon fishing line, a nail, a hammer, and a number of pieces of driftwood. You can buy small screw eyes in a hardware store.

A mobile is a study of form in motion. The one on page 99 is composed of three units. You can make a mobile of as many units as you have time and space for.

Divide your driftwood into two piles. Use pieces that are long and slender as bars or crosspieces. The other pieces may be of a variety of sizes, shapes, and textures. They will be hung from the bars.

Plan or design your mobile before you fasten the pieces into place. Lay out the driftwood on the table. Begin the construction at the bottom and work up to the top. Arrange the bars and the smaller pieces, which will hang from screw eyes set in the bars. As you work, you may find that you want to make some changes in your design.

Find the best place to insert a screw eye in the bottom bar. Sometimes the wood is very hard. To start a hole for the screw eye, first tap a nail part of the way into the wood with a hammer. Then remove the nail, and it will be easy to screw in the eye the rest of the way. Put a screw eye in each of the smaller pieces you plan to hang from this bar.

Hold the bar over a smaller piece, turning the two pieces to find the best angle at which they should be hung and their proper distance apart. Then tie the thread through the bar's screw eye, and fasten it to the screw eye in the piece below. If you are hanging a second piece from this bar, go through the same steps.

Look at the mobile pictured here. You will see that there are two pieces hanging from the bottom bar. One is chunky, the other much narrower. They make a nice contrast.

Now you are ready to attach this unit to the bar above it. Before you fix the screw eye in the top of the lower bar, you must find the point at which it balances. Wrap a string around the bar. The point at which the string holds the bar and its two hanging pieces in perfect balance is the point at which to insert a screw eye.

Mark this point with a pencil.

Insert a screw eye at that point. Attach the bar by thread to a screw eye inserted at any point in the bar above. It can be attached near one end of the bar, and another hanging can be attached at the opposite end, as in the mobile pictured here.

To hang the second bar to a longer one above it, use the string once more. Wrap the string around the second bar. Find the point at which the string balances the bar. Mark it and insert a screw eye in its top.

Follow these steps until you have assembled all the parts of your mobile. Fasten a screw eye in the top bar, and tie a long thread to it. Hold up the mobile by this thread. If you have followed the above steps carefully, all the bars and smaller pieces will be in balance.

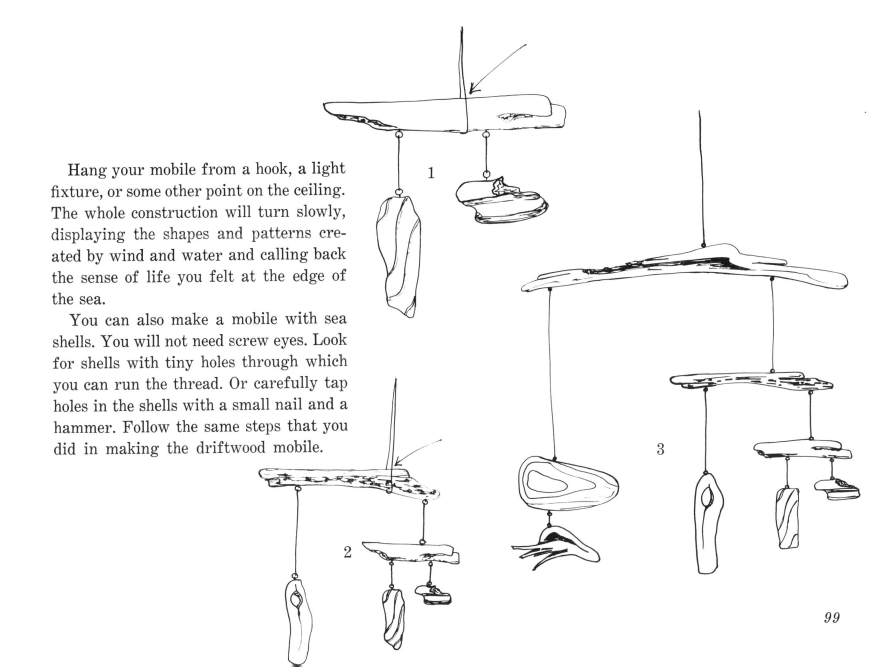

Hang your mobile from a hook, a light fixture, or some other point on the ceiling. The whole construction will turn slowly, displaying the shapes and patterns created by wind and water and calling back the sense of life you felt at the edge of the sea.

You can also make a mobile with sea shells. You will not need screw eyes. Look for shells with tiny holes through which you can run the thread. Or carefully tap holes in the shells with a small nail and a hammer. Follow the same steps that you did in making the driftwood mobile.

1

2

3

99

Sand Painting

Pebbles and Sand

Beaches composed of rocks are on their way to becoming beaches of pebbles and sand. There has not yet been time for the sea to grind them down. The sea is taking its own time.

Every grain of sand you see on the beach has had a long history. Sand was once part of a large slab of rock. Waves and ice fractured the rock. Glaciers ground the rocky pieces into pebbles. The sea rolled the pebbles against one another, rounding and polishing them.

Pebbles that are flattened and smoothed by the sea's violent movement are collectors' items. Their patterns glisten in the water, their rounded edges are cool and soothing to the touch. We can almost feel the restless ocean through the pebbles.

Day after day the sea hurls the pebbles against larger rocks or against one another. It finally grinds them into fine sand. The largest grains are measured in hundredths of an inch, the smallest in thousandths of an inch.

We can tell the kinds of rocks from which the sand came by its color. Dark gray sand beaches came from slate, and red sand beaches from sandstone. The glittering white beaches most of us know were ground from quartz.

No grain of sand remains in any one place for long. It is at the mercy of the wind. If you return in December to a beach you visited in June, it is not the same. The beach and its outlying sandbars have shifted. Wind and water keep sand always on the move.

How to Make Pebble Hot Plates

Starting a collection of surf-polished pebbles and adding to it on every visit to the beach can be an entertaining hobby. The pebbles in themselves are natural treasures. You may want to take some of the most interesting ones from your collection and display them.

This is a long-range project. It will take you five days to make a pebble hot plate.

Choose pebbles with a flat surface. Choose them also for their color, texture, and size. Besides pebbles you will need a package of plain gelatin, a cake pan, plaster of Paris, a glass acrylic medium, and a square piece of felt.

Plain gelatin is sold at grocery stores in packages containing several packets. You will need only half a packet for this project. A layer-cake pan with sloping sides is best because you will be able to remove the hardened plaster of Paris from it more easily. Buy the plaster of Paris in a hardware store. Buy the glass acrylic medium in an art supply store. You can buy the square of felt, which you apply to the bottom of the hot plate, at the sewing supply counter of a department store, dry goods store, or fabric store.

First Day: Grease the cake pan lightly with cooking oil to keep the plaster of Paris from sticking to it when it dries. Mix one half a packet of gelatin, following the instructions on the box. Pour a thin layer (less than one-eighth inch), into the pan.

Lay out your pebbles in a design on the table. Then transfer them in the same design to the bottom of the cake pan. The flattest side of the stones should be laid face down, because the side facing the pan's bottom will be the top of your hot plate. Put the pan, with the pebbles and gelatin, in the refrigerator overnight.

At this point you might ask, "Why gelatin?" The answer is that the gelatin forms a platform for the pebbles. Without the gelatin, the plaster of Paris which you will pour over the pebbles would envelop them. The pebbles would be completely hidden by it.

Second Day: Mix the plaster of Paris, following the directions on the box. Pour it over the pebbles, making sure they are all covered. Set the pan aside for a day to let the plaster harden.

Third Day: Turn over the pan, tap it lightly, and carefully remove the pebble hot plate. Parts of the gelatin will stick to the top of the plate. Wash it off gently with warm water. Pat it dry with a towel and set the plate aside for two days to let it dry thoroughly.

Fifth Day: Cover the bottom of the hot plate with the gloss acrylic medium. Lay the felt over it and trim the edges. Turn the plate over again and rub the stones with baby oil to make them glisten, just as they did in the water. Apply a coat of any dark paint to the rim.

To add a professional touch to your hot plate, apply the gloss acrylic medium to its top and sides. This will give it a lasting finish. It seals the plaster, helps the stones to keep their luster, and makes the hot plate easier to clean.

You will find the finished hot plate well worth the effort you put into making it.

How to Make Sand Paintings

Grains of sand mixed with dry tempera will give you a bright, sparkling painting.

Collect a jar of sand. You will also need dry tempera paint, Elmer's glue, paper cups, and a stiff background such as cardboard or mat board. Buy the dry tempera at an art supply store.

Set out one paper cup for each color you plan to use in your painting. Put a quarter of a cup of sand in each. Then put a different color tempera in each cup. The more tempera you put in, the brighter your color will be. Mix the sand and tempera well.

Make a sketch of your picture on the background board. Let us say that you have decided to paint a flower, as in the sand painting reproduced on page 100.

Draw the outline of the flowers and its leaves. If you want to make the petals yellow, apply glue to each of the petals. Then pour the mixture of sand and yellow tempera over the glue. The mixture will stick only to the petals where you have applied the glue.

Stand the board on its side and tap it to knock off the excess sand. If you want to make the center of the flower orange, brush on some glue. Then pour the mixture of sand and orange tempera over the glue. Again, stand the board on its side and tap off the excess sand. If the leaves are to be green, brush glue on them, then add the mixture of sand and green tempera.

When you have added all the colors, set the painting aside to dry. Tap off whatever excess sand still clings to the surface.

Sea Colander

Algae, Sea Creatures, and Flowering Plants Found at the Shore

ALGAE

Green algae often grow in shallow water. There are many kinds and they are generally smaller than the other algae. Sea lettuce is a common green algae. It is a thin green seaweed resembling the lettuce we eat.

Brown algae include the rockweeds and kelps. Kelp forests grow densely in the Pacific Ocean, with strands as much as one hundred feet long.

Red algae include lava or porphyra, Irish moss, and corallina. They are among the most delicate seaweeds. Porphyra is used in making soups. Irish moss is gathered for many commercial uses.

Green Sea Grass

Irish Moss

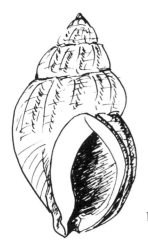

Whelk

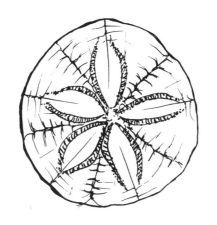

Sand Dollar

SEA CREATURES

Jellyfish have a round disclike body about six inches in diameter. They have long trailing tentacles. They swim by opening and closing the upper disc. Jellyfish are composed mostly of water. Sometimes they are washed up on sandy shores.

Sand dollars have plates or skeletons, em-bossed with a five-petaled pattern, that are often washed up on the shore. When alive, these animals are covered with short movable spines. Their shells or plates are fragile and break easily. Large fish eat sand dollars.

Jingle shells are bright, thin, pearly shells, about one inch in diameter. The hole in the flat shell previously held an anchor cord. The cord is passed through a hole in the flat shell to hold the animal to a rock. The top part of the shell is shaped like a cup. Usually only the flat bottom piece with the hole in it is washed ashore.

Starfish live on clams, mussels, or oysters. They wrap their arms around the shellfish and pull them open. A starfish has a small mouth. It is able to turn its stomach out through its mouth and digest outside its body, the food that otherwise would be too large for it.

Periwinkles are tiny snails with coiled shells. You can find them hidden in the cracks of rocks at the edge of the shore. They eat algae from the rocks. They keep themselves from drying out by closing a tightly fitting trapdoor in their shells.

Barnacles are shrimplike creatures that live in plated shells on rocks near the tide line. A cement they secrete anchors them to the rocks. The pounding surf cannot loosen their hold.

Moonshells are snails with a large "foot." They live in sand and mud. We often see their shells on sandy shores. Even more often we see the circular "sand collar," which holds and protects their eggs.

Shipworms are not really worms but relatives of clams. You will see pieces of driftwood drilled with holes made by the larvae of this mollusk. The shipworms enter the wood as larvae and grow, digging a circular burrow with the edges of their shells.

Tulip Shell

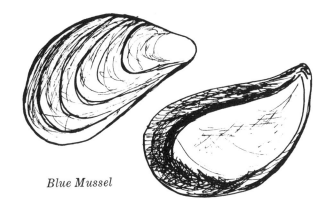

Blue Mussel

Keyhole Limpet

Periwinkle

107

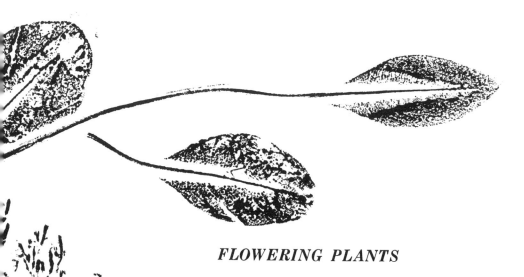

Sea Lavender

FLOWERING PLANTS

Grasses of many kinds grow on sandy dunes and in marshes. The deep roots of sea oats anchor the sand. The mats of intertwined roots in marshes provide nourishment for the leaves of many sea organisms.

Glasswort has thick rubbery branches but very tiny leaves. In the fall it turns red. This salt-resistant plant will grow in very salty soil. It is sometimes picked for salads.

Sea lavender gets its name from the tiny delicate purple blossoms. This plant, growing about one to two feet tall, dries well and can be gathered for winter bouquets.

Beach pea is a trailing, vinelike plant with purple flowers. Its seed pods resemble those you find on garden peas.

Algae

Algae, the basic nutrient of the sea, grow as single cells of microscope size as well as the hundred-foot-long fronds of the giant brown kelp. It is harvested to make countless products, among them aspirin, ice cream, and soups.

The curly fronds or ruffled edges are special designs of these plants to withstand the ocean's great forces. Some fronds are separated into ribbons which part before the waves can rip them or tear them loose.

Algae are simple, primitive plants compared to the more modern plants we have gathered before. None have roots, stems, or leaves as we know them. They absorb carbon dioxide, water, and nutrients through all parts of their surface.

Some algae grow in sheets, others in branches, and others in slabs. Some look extremely leaflike in the water. A few algae have rootlike structures called holdfasts with which they hold themselves on rocks. They are identified by their colors—some green, others brown, others red.

The more primitive small green algae are often found in shallow water, but the long, leathery, brown algae or kelps are products of the deep ocean. They often

Sea Lettuce

break loose and are washed to shore. The reds such as porphyra and Irish moss are among the most delicate of algae and provide excellent subjects for pressing.

How to Press Algae

Algae, collected and pressed, make attractive cards, notepaper, place mats, and pictures. Some, such as sea lettuce and Irish moss, are just the right size for notepaper. The large algae, such as kelp and sea colander, can be matted and covered with plastic paper to make place mats for the table of a summer vacation cottage.

Fill a collecting bucket with sea water and put your algae into it as soon as you gather them. Use the algae as soon as possible. If you keep them overnight, change the water in the bucket.

Assemble drawing paper, twelve inches by eighteen inches, a pan larger than the drawing paper, sea water, newspaper, and paper towels. Cut the drawing paper to size for pressing the smaller algae.

Lay the drawing paper in the pan and cover it with sea water. Float and arrange one of the algae over the paper. Gently lift the paper from the water with the alga on top of it and lay it on the newspaper. Cover it with cheesecloth, more newspapers, and finally several heavy books. Let it dry overnight.

The natural gelatins in the algae will glue them to the paper. If the algae are very heavy, you may have to apply some extra glue to their edges.

Seashore Animals

Seashore animals have no backbones. They breathe, eat, grow, and reproduce in the sea. Often what you see on the beach are only parts of these animals that spent their lives in the ocean. The bottom halves of jingle shells or the circular plates of sand dollars are reminders of the sea's teeming life.

The building blocks of this life are microscopic plankton. These tiny plants and animals provide nourishment for mussels, barnacles, clams, oysters, sand dollars, and many other creatures, which strain the plankton from the water. These plankton strainers, in turn, nourish larger starfish, whelks, crabs, and moon snails.

It is often possible to watch some of these animals at the edge of the tide line

on rocky shores. Creatures live in pools left behind by the tide or cling to rocks, covered and protected by curtains of seaweed. Here you can watch a barnacle swing its hairy legs, beating its tiny cilia in search of food.

Using Flotsam and Jetsam

Shore Collage

Stone, shell, and driftwood collages combine the materials you find on the beach in a handsome composition. Use a weathered driftwood board for a background. Lay out your dried seaweeds, broken shells, parts of animals, and polished stones. Combine them and glue them to the board in a design that will express the life and forces of the shore.

Shore Sculpture

Many objects you find on the shore are interesting enough to be mounted alone. A flat piece of driftwood as a base, a nail, and some Elmer's glue will help you display your treasures. Follow the same steps described for driftwood sculpture.

Shell Collecting

Shells are beautiful in themselves. Shell collecting is a hobby for many people. Most shells fall into one of two large groups. Bivalves are shells with two parts and a hinged opening. Gastropods like sea snails, have a single spiral shell. Mussels, clams, oysters, ark shells, scallops, jingle shells, sea pens, angel wings, and tellins are all bivalves. Whelks, wentletraps, moon snails, slipper shells, periwinkles, cowries, conches, olive shells, and bubble shells are all sea snails. Shells can be used to make mobiles and collages, or they can be mounted as sculptures.

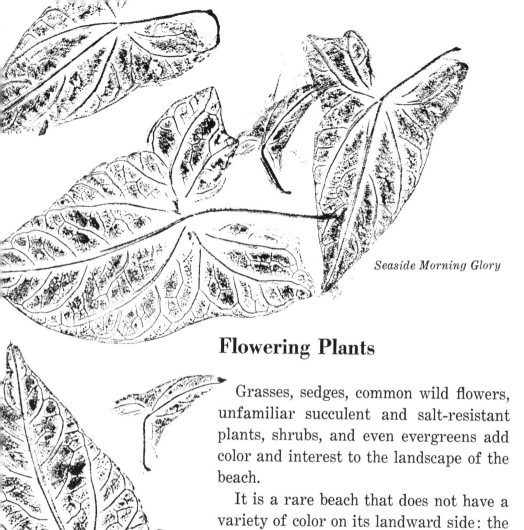

Seaside Morning Glory

Flowering Plants

Grasses, sedges, common wild flowers, unfamiliar succulent and salt-resistant plants, shrubs, and even evergreens add color and interest to the landscape of the beach.

It is a rare beach that does not have a variety of color on its landward side: the yellow of seaside goldenrod, the blues and lavenders of beach pea and sea lavender, the pinks and reds of rugosa roses. These plants have adapted themselves to the harsh conditions of life on the shore—to the salt, wind, sand, and rocks.

Grasses and sedges that grow in sand send down long roots to search for moisture. Succulent plants, such as glasswort, that grow on the salty soils at the edge of the sea have rubbery stems that keep fresh water from evaporating. Other plants grow in the crevices of rocks, probing for the scraps of soil that have lodged there.

Printing Seaside Flowering Plants

The plants shown on page 115 give you

Silverweed

an idea of the variety that can be collected along the shore. Press these plants, following the directions given in Part II. They can be used to decorate postcards, notepaper, place mats and bookmarks. The pressed and mounted plants can also become the basis of a plant collection for use in schools and clubs. After mounting them separately, label each one, giving the plant's name and the date and place of its collection.

The next time you visit the beach, take along your materials for pressing and printing the plants you are sure to find there. Pack plenty of newspapers, your ink, brayer, glass, and paper for printing. Then you will be able to send postcards and notes or even special souvenirs to your friends, who will be aware that they are your own creation. Better still, you will have made a personal record of your experience. Long after the memory of sun, sand, and shells has faded, you will be able to turn to your prints and pressed flowers to re-create the experience of a special time and place.

Beach Pea

115

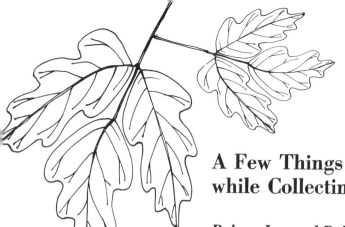

Poison Oak

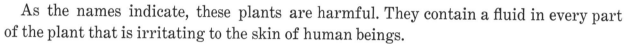

Poison Ivy

A Few Things to Remember while Collecting

Poison Ivy and Poison Oak

As the names indicate, these plants are harmful. They contain a fluid in every part of the plant that is irritating to the skin of human beings.

Poison ivy has shiny leaves, each made up of three leaflets. You will find both poison ivy and poison oak trailing over rocks and climbing tree trunks along roadsides.

If you think you have been exposed to these plants, wash thoroughly with old-fashioned yellow laundry soap. But the best way to avoid the rash is to recognize the plants and not make contact with them.

Rare Plants

When collecting, take only as much material as you plan to use. Some wild flowers are rare, including the lady's slipper, an orchid. A safe rule for collecting flowers that look as though they are unusual is *never* pick them unless they occur abundantly.

Lady's Slipper

Equipment

*A **brayer*** or roller is not expensive. It costs a few dollars. A brayer with a soft rubber
covering distributes ink more evenly than one with a hard vinyl covering.

Printing ink comes in small and large tubes and in several colors. It is washable and
nontoxic. If you plan to use a single tube, black is usually the best choice. One other
color might be red, blue, or green. This ink washes off the glass and your hands with
soap and water.

*A **pane of glass*** should be larger than a sheet of typing paper; nine inches by twelve
inches is a good size. Any hardware store will cut it for you. Cover the edges with
masking tape. This will keep the glass from breaking and keep you from cutting
yourself.

Steps for Printing

Many activities suggested in this book involve printing. It is a simple process. The materials and the steps for printing a leaf are pictured here so that you can become completely familiar with this method of capturing the images of natural things.

Step I: Squeeze some ink on the pane of glass (about as much as the amount of·toothpaste you would use to brush your teeth, or an inch-long ribbon). Roll it in several directions until it sounds sticky. This means the ink is thoroughly distributed and will print well.

Step II: Take your leaf, flower, or grass and place it on the inked glass. Cover with a piece of scrap paper and press it into the ink.

Step III: Lift the leaf and place it on the paper you wish to print. Cover the leaf with a sheet of clear paper. Follow the outline of the leaf through the paper with your fingers, pressing on the stem and veins and following them out to the edges. Lift the top paper and the leaf and examine print.

Aids: If your print is too dark and you cannot see the veins and outline, it means you had too much ink on the glass. Try printing it again. If the print is too faint and all the veins and outlines do not show up, the leaf was not inked thoroughly.

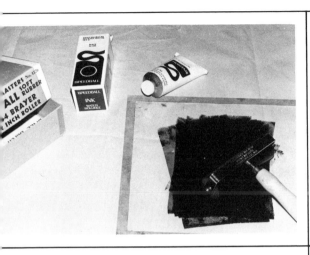

2

3

4

Books You May Want to Read

Keeping the Plants You Pick, by Laura Louise Foster. New York: Thomas Y. Crowell, 1970.

Look at a Flower, by Anne Ophelia Dowden. New York: Thomas Y. Crowell, 1963.

Questions and Answers about Seashore Life, by Ilka Katherine List. New York: Four Winds Press, 1973.

Wild Green Things in the City—A Book of Weeds, by Anne Ophelia Dowden. New York: Thomas Y. Crowell, 1972.

The following Golden Guides (New York: Golden Press) will help you to identify many of the wild things you see or collect: *Insects, Wild Flowers, Trees, Weeds, Fish, Non-Flowering Plants, Sea Shores.*

Index